MW01138972

Reading Poetry with College and University Students

Reading Poetry with College and University Students

Overcoming Barriers and Deepening Engagement

Thomas Fink

BLOOMSBURY ACADEMIC
NEW YORK · LONDON · OXFORD · NEW DELHI · SYDNEY

BLOOMSBURY ACADEMIC
Bloomsbury Publishing Inc
1385 Broadway, New York, NY 10018, USA
50 Bedford Square, London, WC1B 3DP, UK
29 Earlsfort Terrace, Dublin 2, Ireland

BLOOMSBURY, BLOOMSBURY ACADEMIC and the Diana logo
are trademarks of Bloomsbury Publishing Plc

First published in the United States of America 2022

Copyright © Thomas Fink, 2022

For legal purposes the Acknowledgments on pp. 144–146 constitute
an extension of this copyright page.

Cover design by Eleanor Rose
Cover image © Getty Images

All rights reserved. No part of this publication may be reproduced or
transmitted in any form or by any means, electronic or mechanical,
including photocopying, recording, or any information storage or
retrieval system, without prior permission in writing from the publishers.

Bloomsbury Publishing Inc does not have any control over,
or responsibility for, any third-party websites referred to or in this book.
All internet addresses given in this book were correct at the time of
going to press. The author and publisher regret any inconvenience
caused if addresses have changed or sites have ceased to exist,
but can accept no responsibility for any such changes.

Library of Congress Cataloging-in-Publication Data
Names: Fink, Thomas, 1954- author.
Title: Reading poetry with college and university students : overcoming barriers and
deepening engagement / Thomas Fink.
Description: New York : Bloomsbury Academic, 2022. | Includes bibliographical
references and index.
Identifiers: LCCN 2022008910 (print) | LCCN 2022008911 (ebook) |
ISBN 9781501389450 (hardback) | ISBN 9781501389467 (paperback) |
ISBN 9781501389474 (epub) | ISBN 9781501389481 (pdf) | ISBN 9781501389498
Subjects: LCSH: Poetry–Study and teaching (Higher). | Poetry–Explication. |
Poetry–Appreciation. | Poetics.
Classification: LCC PN1101 .F56 2022 (print) | LCC PN1101 (ebook) |
DDC 809.10071/1–dc23/eng/20220511
LC record available at https://lccn.loc.gov/2022008910
LC ebook record available at https://lccn.loc.gov/2022008911

ISBN:	HB:	978-1-5013-8945-0
	PB:	978-1-5013-8946-7
	ePDF:	978-1-5013-8948-1
	eBook:	978-1-5013-8947-4

Typeset by Integra Software Services Pvt. Ltd.
Printed and bound in the United States of America

To find out more about our authors and books visit www.bloomsbury.com
and sign up for our newsletters.

Contents

Introduction

According to Margaret B. Ackerman, "most students come to us with a built-in hostility to poetry. It connotes to them one or more of the following: sentimentality, effeminacy, pretentious diction, circumlocution, and obscurity" (999). She wrote these hefty generalizations a little over a half-century ago, yet in a 2016 doctoral dissertation called "High School English Teachers' Experiences with Poetry Pedagogy," Mary Alice Young seconds Ackerman's points; she finds that "students come to class loaded with antagonistic attitudes toward the genre of poetry, which they often consider sentimental, precious, effeminate, and obscure" (56). Further, Marius Nica makes similar observations about Romanian undergraduates, as Lusvic Torrelas does about Chilean ones.

Mary Alice Young extends the notion of poetry-phobia to teachers: "Many English teachers report failed personal experiences with and/or apathy toward the subject of poetry, while others are discouraged or dissuaded in their pedagogy by their students' poor reactions to the genre" (8). She refers to studies concluding that secondary school teachers believe that they "lack foundational content knowledge, ... or feel ill-prepared to teach poetry themselves." According to Young, their "general fear of poetry" stems from "a lingering sour taste from their individual, academic experiences with the genre, as well as an anxiety about their own expertise" and this "can lead to negative experiences in their current practice" (49). And the teachers tend to transfer their attitudes to their students. Regarding post-secondary classrooms, Alan Golding notes, "For many of our students, ... any poetry beyond what they were force-fed in high school is new," as is "poetry as a *discourse*," and work that professional scholars would not find "innovative … will often produce the effect of newness in neophyte readers: disorientation, bafflement, a sense of readerly inadequacy" (475).

Since at least the 1970s, many writers would contend that poetry hasn't fared well outside academe, either. They claim to hear poetry's death rattle and often blame contemporary poets for obscurity and irrelevant themes, while others have passionately defended the poets and the enduring place of this art in world culture. In his Introduction to *The Best American Poetry 2018*, Dana Gioia observes that "American poetry is currently full of … contradictory trends" (xxv). On the one hand, "the chief way American poets now reach their audience is through readings, either live or transmitted by radio, television, and internet," and "the interest and excitement fostered by the new auditory culture has nurtured a new readership for print poetry." On the other hand, traditional quantification of "conventional literary reading among American adults" (xxiv) and effects of the defunding of the humanities in US universities (xxvi) indicate a serious decline. Denying that there is an "emerging mainstream," Gioia views "the poetry scene" as "a crowded, noisy maternity ward" with "as many competing categories and audience segments as popular music. What plays at Harvard won't get anyone on the dance floor in East Los Angeles, and that's just fine" (xxviii). Well, perhaps those who frequent different dance floors can come to appreciate, if not prefer, each other's moves.

Stephanie Burt makes the refreshing point in *Don't Read Poetry* (2019) that the genre and judgments about it are too diverse to be reduced to a simple, unified set of generalizations. In lieu of generalizing, she argues, one should engage with specific features of actual poems. This is, in fact, the message of the book's arresting title. Burt asserts that there are six qualities of poems that have mainly attracted readers. Some readers focus on one or two, some on more, and few are equally concerned with all. Burt's categories are feeling, characters, forms, difficulty, wisdom, and community.

This list covers a lot of ground. It can be helpful to Burt's primary audience—those who aren't sure but would like to get a sense of what reading poems might do for them—and perhaps even as a jumping-off point for an introduction to poetry course. As she states, multiple categories can simultaneously entice a reader. Further, I'd like to stress that various categories are *embedded* in one another. Don't readers associate "feeling"—the main focus of my second chapter—and the "characters" who "feel" (and remind readers of their own feelings)? Since feeling and thinking are profoundly connected, a quest for "wisdom" in poetry connects with affect. In fact, one might pursue wisdom about how to process feeling. Encounters with characters in poems can provide wisdom about oneself and about actual interactions with others.

The chapter that follows takes up "difficulty" as a problem for many readers of poetry, but I thoroughly agree with Burt that it intrigues other readers and can even motivate some who initially resist it after they work through barriers. "Difficulty" is intimately bound up with "feeling," as well as "forms," "wisdom," and "community." The opportunity to progress from frustration to a grasp of compelling *emotional* complexity often motivates my students who have pursued difficult literary texts. Challenging "forms" can make one think about effects of material properties of language and how they influence meaning-making. And through metacognition (thinking about one's thinking and perception), "wisdom" might arise. Some see themselves as members of a "community" who believe that a particular kind of "difficult" poetry aptly expresses their social interests. As a goal of poetic engagement, "community" depends on exploration of feelings—for example, about power relations within a society, as well as about the nature of "wisdom." Poets also frequently explore how formal choices influence community-building. They also present characters as exemplary figures for or against a community's development of identity and solidarity.

Would you like to hear a long, breathless sermon about why *everyone* should read poems consistently for the rest of their lives? I didn't think so. Regardless of what anyone tells them, many people won't stick with poetry after their English courses, and they'll survive the self-deprivation. My goal in these pages is to foreground ways in which dialogues about poems in a college/university English class or a professor's office or a student cafeteria or online chat can become more meaningful, productive, and engaged. I'm confident that faculty can motivate and guide college students to identify and surmount difficulties they encounter with poems, help them capitalize on the emotional benefits of reading poetry, and foster their ability to think carefully about differing interpretations of a single poem. And if class sessions are dynamic, more students will write essays on poetry that demonstrate solid aesthetic consciousness, the capacity to pose a problem clearly and aptly and then solve it, meaningful application of research to interpretation, metacognitive awareness, and the ability to integrate knowledge about poetry with what they learn in other courses and in daily life.

1

Barriers to Access and Engagement

About twenty years ago, I was having dinner with a family friend. He told me that he was impressed with the fact that I wrote criticism of poetry, since he considered it the most difficult genre. The gentleman, a professor of Slavic Languages at UCLA, happened to be one of the leading translators of Eastern European fiction. Even *he*—a translator of innovative twentieth-century novels—seemed to subscribe to the idea that poetry poses greater challenges than literary prose. It was far from the first or last time I've heard this kind of comment.

Joshua Marie Wilkinson nicely captures the impatience that some people feel with poetry's difficulty: "When we ask what a poem is about, this tends … to be shorthand for, *ok, ok, but tell me what it means*; in other words, just reduce its helter-skelter language to something I can *get* … I haven't got all day here." Likening poetic meaning to that of music, Wilkinson asserts that "our inability to answer that question succinctly is hardly a testament to the meaninglessness of poetry," but rather an instance of the questioner mistaking "a poem for a newspaper article or even an anecdote," which causes "expectations for a poem's language [to change]—drastically."

Should a search for authorial **intention** guide the process of interpretation of a poem (or any literary text)? This question is a good place to start our scrutiny of difficulty. For a thorough summary of the many definitions and subcategories of intention, one can consult Sally Bushell's article "Intention Revisited." I find Michael Hancher's 1972 article, "Three Kinds of Intention," especially useful for sorting out issues of intention in poetry. First, he speaks of "programmatic intention," which involves "the purpose(s) for writing a literary text in a particular genre" (829). This could also include choices of subgenre features such as the use of traditional European meter, free verse, other rhythmic or sonic constraints, and prose blocks or paragraph. Next, Hancher defines "active intention" as designating "the actions that the author, at the time that he [*sic*] finishes his text, understands himself to be performing in that text" (830). "active intention" involves the author's understanding of the meaning of a poem's passages and the text as a whole. Thirdly, "final intention" has to do with "caus[ing] something or other to happen" (829). It concerns effects to be produced, such as "to cause in [the] reader a change of knowledge or belief about some matter; or to cause that reader to laugh or chuckle or smile, or to cause him [*sic*] to undergo a catharsis of pity or fear" (834–835). He adds that an author's final intentions might be entirely personal—for example, pecuniary or psychotherapeutic. For the purposes of my discussion here, both active and final intention are most relevant.

In the interpretation of poetry, readers frequently link the gauging of authorial intention with discernment of **tone**. In an article on tone, Langdon Hammer considers "tone in a poem … roughly analogous to … a person's mood"; the reader interprets "some putative interiority on the basis of gestures and signs, through which we ascribe authorial intention …" (76). Therefore, for him, tone marks "the manner of relationship the writer constructs with his reader," and Hammer approvingly cites I. A. Richards's assertion that authorial intention located in tone may be unconscious as well as conscious. Hammer seems to believe that discovering this "interiority" is the "essence" of interpretation. According to Hammer, while tone in actual speech involves "inflection or timbre"—"a combination of pitch … and stress" indicating "the pattern that determines whether a sentence will be heard as (for example) a question or a statement, as well as which words in it will be emphasized and to what effect"—tone gleaned from "the poem on the page" is "intangible" (76). Since it is "a figure for effects of voice we can imagine but never hear," readers have to be attentive to such features as line-breaks (i.e. enjambments) and typographical components, such as italics.

Ellen Bryant Voigt also explains the difficulties of understanding tone in poetry on the page. Stressing how "most of us can identify tone in *life*," sometimes just to survive, Voigt states that "we reconstruct the emotional content," not only from pitch and stress, but from "volume, … pacing, and rhythmic pattern of speech …" (78). In her view, which connects tone and musicality, "any single element does not contain" tone, but "what's important is the combination of elements" (84) that readers simultaneously experience with "an event or idea verbalized, cast into discursive logic" (89). "This simultaneity" is responsible for the difficulty of pinpointing "the source of tone in a poem," as well as readers' efforts to use "the linear or discursive logic of language" (89–90) to characterize it.

As sensible as their ideas sound, Hammer and Voigt do not confront whether authorial intention is really accessible or not and whether its representation by a reader can ever stand as a true, complete interpretation. In "The Intentional Fallacy," an extremely influential essay originally published in 1946, the New Critic William K. Wimsatt and his philosopher/aesthetician colleague Monroe C. Beardsley deny the first two of these possibilities. They argue that "design or intention" should not be "a *standard* by which the critic is to judge the worth of the poet's performance" (3). Two decades later, in "Genesis: A Fallacy Revisited," Wimsatt clarifies that he and Beardsley are not merely talking about evaluation: "The design or intention of the author is neither available nor desirable as a standard for judging either the meaning or the value of a work of literary art" (222).

Regarding interpretation, Wimsatt and Beardsley distinguish between "internal evidence," obtained "through the semantics and syntax of a poem, through our habitual knowledge of the language, through grammars, dictionaries and all the literature which is the source of dictionaries, in general through all that makes a language and culture," and "external evidence," which might include "revelations (in journals … or letters or reported conversations) about how or why the poet wrote the poem" (9) to or about a person, place, or situation relevant to the work. In addition, though, they speak of "an intermediate kind of evidence about the character of the author or about private or semiprivate meanings attached to words or topics by an author or [his/her] coterie." But they caution that these three kinds of evidence, especially the latter two, "shade into one another ... subtly," and so distinguishing between them can be difficult. If Wimsatt and Beardsley concede that a reader can apply the author's or his/her coterie's "semiprivate meanings" to an analysis, then they are also admitting that authorial intention is *partly* available through "external evidence," such as other texts that confirm that the writer associates particular words with these meanings.

Wimsatt asserts in "Genesis: A Fallacy Revisited" that "the closest one could ever get to the artist's intending or meaning mind, outside his work, would be still short of his *effective* intention or *operative* mind as it appears in" the text (221–222). Sally Bushell holds that Wimsatt is saying that "it is safer to stick with what you can see and know (the poem) than to speculate about what you do not know (the author's mind)" (64). However, as Annabel Patterson observes, Wimsatt and Beardsley's original "essay assume[s] that public and objective standards of evaluation [are] at least conceivable" and are most effective if they minimize the role of authorial subjectivity, but these scholars do not raise "the problem of the *critic's* subjectivity and how it might be substituted (or mistaken) for public standards ..." (141).

Although poststructuralist theorists critique intentionalism, they do this from an extremely different perspective than Wimsatt and Beardsley. Roland Barthes's "The Death of the Author" credits Mallarmé with the insight that "it is language which speaks, not the author; to write is ... to reach that point where only language acts, 'performs,' and not 'me'" (143). Barthes in this frequently hyperbolic 1967 polemic and/or satire dismisses the idea that "a text is ... a line of words releasing a single 'theological' meaning (the 'message' of an Author-God)"; he sees it as "a multi-dimensional space in which a variety of writings, none of them original, blend and clash," "a tissue of quotations drawn from the innumerable centres of culture" (146). He opposes textual analysis "sought in" the author, as though the work "were always in the end, through the more or less transparent allegory of the fiction, the voice of a single person, the *author* 'confiding' in us" (143), and he declares that "once the Author is removed, the claim to decipher a text becomes quite futile" (147). To put it perhaps too neatly, for Barthes, the signifying play of language exceeds any conjecture about the author's intention; he recognizes the reader as the "location" where this play can occur.

In an essay published two years after Barthes's text, Michel Foucault also challenges belief in "the author" as "an indefinable source of significations which fill a work" and "a certain fundamental principle by which, in our culture, one limits, chooses, and excludes," impeding "the free circulation, the free manipulation, the free composition, decomposition, and recomposition of fiction" ("What Is an Author?" 119). Instead of hunting for intention, he engages in scholarship that examines "the author-function" (108) in order to analyze "the subject as a variable and complex function of discourse" (118) that reflects the circulation of power in a social realm. Jacques Derrida does not suggest that "the category of intention" should "disappear" in the reading of philosophy or literature but that "it will no longer be able to govern the entire scene and the entire system of utterances" because language functions as "chains of iterable [repeatable] marks" (*Margins of Philosophy*, 326). The author cannot control this repetition of units of language to impose a particular conscious intention. Since "the writer writes *in* a language and *in* a logic whose proper system, laws, and life his discourse by definition cannot dominate absolutely," to some degree, s/he is "governed by the system" (*Of Grammatology* 158). Derrida is interested in the "relationship, unperceived by the writer, between what he [*sic*] commands and what he does not command of the patterns of the language that he uses." The word "always" does not account for situations in which what lies outside a particular author's intention is trivial. However, since the poststructuralists began to influence US literature departments in the 1970s, this "hermeneutics of suspicion" (a phrase coined but not particularly endorsed by Paul Ricoeur in *Freud and Philosophy*) has long been a major dimension of the work of deconstructive, feminist, queer, Marxist, postcolonial, and ecological theorists who disclose authors' lack of awareness of or resistance to ideological implications of their texts' discourse and of what that discourse excludes.

Various forms of psychological criticism tend to find meaning in the text beyond the author's conscious intention. In literary studies, the most influential (but most slippery) version of Freudian psychoanalysis has been Jacques Lacan's linguistically inflected "return to Freud." Speaking of a subject divided or split between consciousness and the unconscious, Lacan identifies "the unconscious" as "that part of concrete discourse qua transindividual, which is not at the subject's disposal in reestablishing the continuity of his [*sic*] conscious discourse" (214); it is "the censored chapter" that is "marked by a blank or occupied by a lie …" (215). "Starting with Freud," Lacan states, "the unconscious becomes a chain of signifiers that repeats and insists somewhere (on another stage or in a different scene, as he wrote), interfering in the cuts offered it by actual discourse and the cogitation it informs" (676). Since Lacan finds that "the truth … has already been written elsewhere" (215), he asserts that it can be recuperated. Perhaps a tracing of the metonymic chain in the psychoanalytic process is roughly analogous to the attempt to articulate the dynamics of an author or speaker's unconscious in a poem, but separating the work of conscious intention and the elements of that chain may be extremely difficult.

As Barthes does in "The Death of the Author," those who want to avoid endorsing authorial intention as a basis for interpretation often use personification to describe the text or language. For example, in an essay on difficulty in poetry, Reginald Shepherd speaks of "difficulties interpreting tone, determining the stance and attitude the poem takes and wants the reader to take toward its material." Hancher explains that those who refer "to the 'intention' of 'the work itself'" are presenting "a critical fiction," since "no text really 'means' in and of itself" (850).

In his catalogue poem, "This Poem," Tom Beckett has his speaker repeatedly utilize the "critical fiction" of personification that ascribes intention to the poem itself as he explores issues that various theorists discussed above have raised about intention. Here are the poem's opening tercets: "This poem/ Proffers/ Its ass.// This poem/ Penetrates me" (7). If one reads the speaker as a stand-in for the poet, s/he may surmise that the poet is acting as a ventriloquist—that he is doing the proffering of either seduction, his own vulnerability, or derogation, but using personification to mask it. On the other hand, the passage could mean that the poem features seductive language, or (if "proffer" is taken ironically) that the text is vulnerable to negative assessment, or that some of its words insult its audience. In this second scenario, the poet does *not* assert that he has actively intended seductive or insulting words or tried to make himself vulnerable to attack. Instead, "the poem" is a site where readers can bring conventional understandings of speech acts to arrive at any of the interpretations that I have mentioned.

"This poem/ Multiplies" (13) in the sense that audience members make "this poem" fit the contexts that they assign to it. Let's suppose that the poet finally intends to show respect for the audience, but a linguistic ambiguity s/he hadn't noticed is taken in a way that offends a reader. Because readers can process language in ways that the author can't control, the poem can "moon" its writer. But also, the poet might feel undermined by his own wayward unconscious if a reader makes him aware of it. This can have a negative psychological impact on ("penetrate") the writer, though "me" might only refer to a speaker, even a particular reader. Yet a poet is also a reader whose own (revised) interpretation, beyond even his active and final intentions, can make him aware of something disquieting about himself that he would rather not have had to confront. The poet can even experience masochistic pleasure about the poem's textual aggression against his concept of himself.

Various tercets in "This Poem" pertain to the reflection about the poem's identity and, in one case, the poet's:

This poem
Eschews
The copula ... (8)

This poem
Stares into
A mirror.

This poem
Plays
With itself. (11)

Only the poet, not the poem, can decide whether or not to employ a form of the verb "to be" and thereby encourage or discourage linkages that evince some sort of identity. "Copula" is not readable only as a grammatical label here, and the first tercet above is followed by "This poem/ Is fucked" (8). So in the translation of the first personification into more literal possibilities, the speaker can be read as alleging that the poem includes no copular verbs, which is manifestly untrue, as in "This Poem/ Is an/ Empty/ Container" (12), and that the poem's language does not represent sexual union, which seems to be contradicted immediately. From another perspective, though, the "poem/ Eschews/ The copula" because a signifier fails to achieve the full presence of a signified, as Derrida and Lacan remind us in their different ways. When a poet uses mimesis to try to provoke an emotional response in the reader, the latter may not recognize the imitation.

In the second tercet above, the personification reverses the notion that a poem is supposed to be a kind of "mirror" rather than using one. Although a poem has no eyes, poetic language can contain references to its own functioning as poetry, as language, or as representation in general, as in this "metapoem." Is a poet needed to intend this metapoetic gesture programmatically or actively, or is such metapoetic reference built into the discourse—in Barthes's sense, language "speaking" its own status as well as "performing"? Even if the latter is so, it takes a reader to notice what's happening. And, even if only the poet can "stare" as a proxy for the poem, each reader acts as a "mirror" in which the poem is reflected. To echo a tenet of reader-response criticism, an unread poem is inert. It has a diminished identity: without such human "mirrors," the poem's "identities" cannot be activated. In the ambiguous ultimate tercet above, the poet could be ventriloquizing to hide his "shameful" verbal masturbation and his poetic manipulations of his identity-construct. However, the stanza could also indicate how verbal play involving polysemy, which disrupts any unity of meaning in the poem, is beyond the author's intentions in delimiting "communication," as Barthes, Foucault, and Derrida suggest.

"This Poem" ends: "This poem/ Pretends not/ To know me" (13). It is only the second time that "me," the only personal pronoun used, appears in the poem, and the first was in the second tercet. I will assume for now that the author is "me." If I translate the personification into something "sensible" by making the verb "pretends" connote "seems" and "know" connote "be influenced by," then the speaker claims that the text's language may seem *but is not* totally independent of the author's intentions. Then again, there is no internal evidence that "me" is the poet; it could refer to a generic speaker—or even a reader. A text can appear self-sufficient, needing neither the input of the one who wrote its words nor the one who reads them. Throughout the poem, Beckett's tropes, images, and abstractions call attention to the interpenetration of the variable impacts of authorial intention, textuality, and the reader's activity.

There are many cases in which it is indispensable to consider authorial intention, because external evidence is extremely compelling. In particular poems by avowedly political authors, active and final intention may not be the *sole* determinant of meaning, but without considering them, what chance is there for someone to read cogently? For example, when the speaker near the end of Mahmoud Darwish's long poem "Mural" declares, "What was mine: my yesterday./ What will be mine: the distant tomorrow,/ and the return of the wandering soul as if nothing had happened" (161), the lines and the entire poem must be associated with the poet's protest against the Israeli government's denial of land and sovereignty to the Palestinian people and his "defiant call of reclamation, resistance and return" (Hamamra and Abusamra 1078). Any attempt to apply a general theological meaning to the notion of possession ("mine") and dispossession and to "the wandering soul" rather than the reference to the diasporic situation of Palestinians will cloud the political exigency of Darwish's intentions, which can even be found in his love poems. The very structure of Gloria E. Anzaldúa's 1987 book *Borderlands/La Frontera—the New Mestiza* provides some insurance that readers will take the author's active and final political intentions seriously. Her strategy is to intersperse prose essays on the history of the Mexican region, the relationship between Mexico and the United States, the oppression of ChicanX people since the Mexican-American War (including autobiographical material), and the marginalization of lesbians and gays within her own people with poems such as "To live in the *Borderlands* means you" (195) that are intended to reflect and challenge these concrete historical situations.

When external evidence is not so clearly identifiable, I try to guide students who are pursuing conscious intention to understand the provisional, partial nature of what they are attempting. If they think that the poet "is" the speaker, or in the case of a poem with multiple voices, one of the speakers, they need to make some effort to give precise external evidence for that conclusion. Their analytic process may lead them to believe at times that a writer's final intentions are not unified like a "thesis" but multiple. Most of the time, they should be dissuaded from using language in an essay that claims either that intention is the "key" to the poem or that the one that they have found is the totality of what the poet must have meant. I want students to recognize that, at best, they can make a strong conjecture about an author's active and final intention. Further, the essay's conclusion is a good place to situate the writer's thoughts about whatever problems of interpretation conscious intention can't resolve.

If a student hopes to reveal traces of the author or speaker's unconscious, s/he contrasts these findings with his/her sense of conscious intentions, sometimes gleaned from an author's statement about intentions or with a previous critical account bolstered by external evidence. Neuroscientists are still in early stages of using exciting new technology to determine how consciousness and the unconscious work in areas of the human brain, and there is no consensus among psychological theorists about the reading of the unconscious through textual means or dream interpretation. (Also, a writer's statement of intention can be misleading or inaccurate for self-serving reasons, though others can't prove this.) Students who try to locate unconscious traces in a poem will need to recognize that they develop a set of conjectures based on an interpretive framework that lacks the status of scientific "law." The best they can expect is a relatively convincing set of assertions.

A reader engaged in an ideologically motivated "hermeneutics of suspicion" would posit some strand of authorial intention, whether conscious or unconscious, in order to show how external evidence, such as a feminist theoretical construct or concrete historical circumstances, frames internal evidence. The goal is not necessarily, as in New Critical close reading and in some psychoanalytic interpretations, to perform an exhaustive inventory of plausible meanings in the poem but to concentrate on a substantial portion of the text that is relevant to the reader's sociopolitical or philosophical concerns. A student may also discern a divided intention, one aspect of which occasions negative critique and the other which gains the interpreter's approval.

When a reader wants to bypass intention (including unconscious intention) altogether, external evidence in the form of intertextual connections will probably be necessary. An author can programmatically and finally intend meaning to proliferate without certain conventional restrictions and thus to subvert ordinary kinds of intention. Later in this chapter, I will be more specific about this in discussing several forms of difficulty, such as semantic deviation. For now, I will just cite Charles Bernstein's sense of "poetry and poetics" as "letting language find ways of meaning through [him]" rather than "mak[ing] words mean something [he] want[s] to say" (*My Way* 26); Bernstein advocates "performing and responding to overlapping meanings" while "reading poetry" rather than pursuing "the goal of deciphering a fixed, graspable meaning" (*Attack of the Difficult Poems* 48). In writing an essay, a student who is not discussing intention may choose to resort to personification to relay what the poem "says," or s/he might use an

"I" statement: ("I read the trope of '_____' as indicating _____"). When a single speaker is presumed, one can attribute action or thought to "the speaker" without reference to the poet. A student-critic can also state how s/he thinks multiple signifying elements relate to one another (without reference to anyone).

Since we cannot locate a realm where an author's "true" full intention or an "objective" unity of intention and global meaning exists, the best we can achieve are well-constructed arguments that permit vibrant, specific conversations among those holding differing perspectives.

Now I'll turn to seven further areas of difficulty that poetry can pose for readers: allusion, ambiguity, narrative (in)coherence, vocabulary, semantic deviation (including tropes), syntactic deviation, and categorization (of a text as poetry or not).

An inability to catch **allusion** in poetry can prevent readers from grasping specific geographical, cultural, political, economic, or conceptual information that might serve as crucial external evidence of a poet's active or final intentions. Onondaga/Mic Mac poet Gail Tremblay's "Crow Voices," a poem contrasting the "speech" and activities of clever, purposeful crows in two different areas of the United States, ends with an allusion to a Native American myth about the being who enabled the sun to warm earth dwellers: "Inside the rain forest,/ crows act serious, whispering about enemies,/ about food supplies, about how Raven/ stole their wit when he proved/ he was so clever he could take the sun" (21). If readers don't track this allusion and merely assume that Tremblay uses a surreal trope for a splendid achievement, they miss a chance to learn about an interesting detail of Native American culture and how it fits the poem's treatment of intergroup competition involving creativity and collective survival.

Yusef Komunyakaa's poem "Hanoi Hannah," first published in 1988 and revised slightly when it appeared in his *Pleasure Dome: New and Collected Poems* (2001), is a prime example of a densely allusive text. All of the allusions refer to the specifics of the war in Vietnam and of sixties music. The poem juxtaposes the title-character's words, soldiers' reactions to them, and the sights and sounds of jungle warfare:

Ray Charles! His voice
calls from waist-high grass,
& we duck between gray sandbags.
"Hello, Soul Brothers. Yeah,
Georgia's also on my mind."
Flares bloom over the trees.
"Here's Hannah again.
Let's see if we can't
light her goddamn fuse
this time." Artillery
shells carve a white arc
against dusk. Her voice rises
from a hedgerow on our left. (198)

The title, "Hanoi Hannah," refers to the name that US soldiers aiding the South Vietnamese against the Communist North in Vietnam's civil war gave Trinh Thi Ngo (1931–2016), who, on the broadcasts, called herself "Thuo Huong" ("autumn fragrance"). She "served the Communist cause over the radio waves" through her "Voice of Vietnam" radio program. Ngo "enticed homesick [US] troops," including POWs like future Senator John McCain, "with music," especially folk, rock, and soul with an antiwar message, and then "read scripts, prepared by North Vietnamese officials, that chronicled American battlefield defeats, as well as antiwar activity and social upheaval at home" (Langer) to emphasize the abject futility and injustice of the soldiers' efforts and the idea that their government was exploiting them. She was urging them to defect.

Even without the historical context, a reader can guess that Hanoi Hannah's voice is coming from a radio and can understand that the antagonism between the soldiers and her is related to a war. But without certain elements of that context, a good deal of the poem's psychological complexity is missed. It is telling that Komunyakaa alludes to two major African-American performers, Ray Charles and Tina Turner, as the sole evidence of Ngo's playlist, rather than including a white protest singer like Bob Dylan or Joan Baez. Hanoi Hannah alludes to Ray Charles's song "Georgia on My Mind" while directly addressing black soldiers ("Soul Brothers") to debilitate them by making them nostalgic for home. ("Georgia" is an especially useful proper name here, as it can signify either the southern state or a woman.) Ngo also plays on soldiers' sexual insecurities: "'It's Saturday night in the States./ Guess what your woman's doing tonight./ I think I'll let Tina Turner/ tell you, you homesick GIs" (198). Later, by serving as the person to inform them of Martin Luther King Jr.'s assassination by a white supremacist, she implicitly reminds African-American soldiers that they were sent by President Lyndon Johnson's government to sacrifice their lives in Vietnam, where "waist high grass" and other woefully unfamiliar conditions hamper their ability to fight, while racism continues to oppress their people at home:

> "You know you're dead men,
> don't you? You're dead
> as King today in Memphis.
> Boys, you're surrounded by
> General Tran Do's division."
> Her knife-edge song cuts
> deep as a sniper's bullet.
> "Soul Brothers, what you dying for?" (198)

One hopes that, without prompting, students will recognize "King" here as the great civil rights leader and will know that he was assassinated in Memphis, Tennessee, but this cannot be taken for granted. The soldier quoted as wanting to "light [Hanoi Hannah's] goddamn fuse" expresses hostility to the broadcaster's messages. The synesthetic phrase "knife-edge song" and the simile comparing it to "a sniper's bullet" show how intensely the listeners are disturbed by Ngo's information about the unprecedented resistance to the war and continued racial unrest. (Interestingly, she acquired this data from mainstream US media.) It is important to think about *why* they are so rattled by a voice on a radio, especially since they face tremendous *physical* danger all the time.

In an interview about his experience as an "information specialist" (reporter) alongside the troops on Vietnam battlefields, Komunyakaa notes that "in an ambush," the combatants "didn't have time to think about" political issues, since they "were keenly sensitive to surviving"; they understood the importance of "try[ing] to protect your fellow soldiers, black or white," yet "there were those vicious arguments with one's self. One would feel divided" (Baer 9–10). In another interview he speaks of "problems exist[ing] between American soldiers … when they were drinking and trying to forget the war and elements of the war … Then the real American shows up again" (Alleyne). Komunyakaa speaks of how the Vietnamese were aware of turmoil "in the American psyche when it came to race, and sometimes they expertly played up on it"; he cites "the idea of Hanoi Hannah" as a good example: "Her voice penetrated. … You know, that gets your attention when you're out in the middle of nowhere."

In line with external evidence that these comments provide, and with my sense of various other Vietnam poems that appear in the same 1988 collection, I read a substantial part of Komunyakaa's active intention in "Hanoi Hannah" primarily as a depiction—accomplished without the speaker's "editorial" intervention—of African-American soldiers' severe cognitive dissonance while sandwiched between US military propaganda/indoctrination and Ngo's counterpropaganda. Part of the rage against Hanoi Hannah is their realization that much of what she is saying is tragically and infuriatingly valid. The poem's concluding sentence suggests that guilt about the massive destruction of Vietnamese lives and land caused by US involvement in the civil war may be channeled into part of that rage: "Her voice grows flesh/ & we can see her falling/ into words, a bleeding flower" (198). If students are interested in the subject matter after the professor introduces "Hanoi Hannah" as a poem about war, they may be willing to use a search engine to track down a host of allusions and pay close attention to how the allusions create context for an understanding of the poem. If the subject matter doesn't grab them, they might tune out, but allusion-tracking can be a useful and potentially engaging group activity prior to full class discussion.

Allusions may pose another kind of challenge than the ones I have described. Sometimes, readers differ in the allusions they locate and consider relevant for understanding a text. W.B. Yeats's poem "A Prayer for My Daughter" provides a trenchant example of this form of disagreement, as I'll demonstrate in my third chapter. Further, critics differ in the weight that they give to the influence of intertextual alignments in the overall analysis, and even when they concur in the identification of specific allusions, they often interpret their significance differently.

When allusions are not intrinsic to the reading as a whole (except for students who choose to do a research paper), an instructor can supply general background information in advance to motivate a class to concentrate on other more accessible aspects of the poem and later de-emphasize the tracking of allusions. In her enthusiastic introduction to Eliot's *The Waste Land*, Mary Karr holds that a precise grasp of the poem's myriad allusions is unnecessary and that "95 percent of its splendor exists on the surface ... ." She finds poet's "notes ... both capricious and shifting in both purpose and attitude," as "there isn't much constancy to what gets a note and what doesn't." Discerning self-mockery in his tone, she believes that Eliot considered the notes "trivial."

Karr stresses how *The Waste Land* can elicit a powerful emotional response if one is aware of the general historical context, especially in major urban centers; she speaks of the text as "somewhat disparate pieces assembled to create in readers the kind of despair that infected much of Western Europe after the Great War," an event of "wholesale motorized murder ... part and parcel of the increasingly mechanized world that had been assembling since the first cotton gins and mills marked the Industrial Revolution." She likens the poem's collage surfaces to the heterogeneity of cities. Karr persuasively indicates how a professor in some circumstances might be able to circumvent students' anxiety about highly allusive poems.

Ambiguity, a major aesthetic resource for some readers, can be a stumbling block for others. William Empson's 1949 *Seven Types of Ambiguity* is the modern "classic" analysis of the ambiguous in literature. Empson's discussions of actual poems in the book seem far more intricate than his descriptions of the types, but I will stick here with some mention of the types. The first is metaphor, since it contains two elements that are not necessarily connected. (But metaphor is important enough to be treated, along with other tropes, extensively in a separate part of this chapter.) Empson speaks of the "second type ... in word or syntax occur[ring] when two or more meanings are resolved into one" (48). In the third type, "two ideas, which are connected only by being both relevant in the context, can be given one word simultaneously" (102). I view these two cases as extremely similar: in each, an interpreter's success in making disparate meanings cohere depends on an ability to take words/phrases from different contexts and to locate a third context that includes both.

Empson's fourth, fifth, and seventh types invoke knowledge of conscious authorial intention, which is not necessarily accessible. However, the fourth, "two or more meanings of a statement do not agree among themselves, but combine to make clear a more complicated state of mind in the author" (133), is similar to the notion of contextual unification in the second and third; it makes sense if one leaves out the author's "state of mind" and thinks of the example of the reader interpreting a passage as a paradox or reconciliation of opposites, the kind of poetic analysis privileged by the New Critics. The fifth type involves "the author ... discovering his idea in the act of writing, or not holding it all in his mind at once," and Empson uses the example of "a simile which applies to nothing exactly, but lies half-way between two things when the author is moving from one to the other" (155). Again, is it really possible to assess whether the author is "discovering" anything or presenting a succession of ideas or images over which s/he has scant conscious control or just having his/her speaker imitate a process of discovery? One might argue that the "half-way" simile does not indicate progress from one point to another but instead places the two elements next to one another so that the relation can be interpreted. (Empson acknowledges that "the degree to which the apprehension of the ambiguity must be conscious" [48] is variable.) In my view, the effect of this kind of juxtaposition is too far from other types to be classified as ambiguity.

The seventh type seems to be the opposite of the reconciliation ostensibly achieved in the fourth: "two opposite meanings defined by the context" make "the total effect ... show a fundamental division in the writer's mind" (192). Whether or not the author consciously or unconsciously experiences such a division, a reader can conclude that the opposites, as represented in the text, cannot be reconciled. S/he can either accept, appreciate, or learn from the situation of unresolved ambiguity or find it an aesthetic, political, psychological, or philosophical failure of the poem. The sixth type involves "a statement" that "says nothing, by tautology, by contradiction, or by irrelevant statements, so that the reader is forced to invent statements" that might "conflict with one another" (176). Though underscoring the reader and not authorial intention, this type also points to cases when the poem's language does not permit (or seem to permit) an interpreter's unification of the elements of ambiguity through the location of a new context. In presenting the sixth and seventh types, Empson seems close to characterizing a deconstructive undecidability or aporia. Barbara Johnson speaks of "Mallarmé's famous obscurity" involving "his radical transformation of intelligibility itself through the ceaseless production of seemingly mutually exclusive readings of the same piece of language ... Reference is here not denied but suspended" (65).

I've suggested that two of Empson's seven types should be consigned to other categories and that presumptions about authorial intention should not structure differences among the types. So I'll compound my audacity by suggesting that the other five can be pragmatically reduced to two, with a third that Empson does not directly mention but is common in worldly decision-making. First, the reader is able to apply multiple meanings of a word, phrase, or other passage so that they fit into a particular context; second, the reader cannot find a context to "enclose" multiple meanings; third, the reader selects one of the multiple meanings as relevant to the interpretive context and assumes that others do not fit.

Several things can go wrong when one meets with ambiguity. Sometimes, a reader suspects that ambiguity is present but has difficulty envisioning a new context that can align the multiple possibilities—until, with luck, someone else comes along to supply that context. Another problem occurs when a reader finds a single meaning in a word and does not perceive an ambiguity that others do; this may limit the fullness of his/her reading. In the Welsh seventeenth-century metaphysical poet George Herbert's "Christmas (1)," the speaker is a traveler who has experienced various pleasures and, now weary and apparently ashamed of himself, stops at an inn, only to encounter his "dearest Lord," whom he addresses in the poem's last sentence as the one "whose glorious, yet contracted light,/ Wrapt in night's mantle, stole into a manger …" (85). A typical way of glossing this passage is to say that God the Father illuminated the nativity of Jesus in the manger with light that is reduced in scale, but it is also possible to read the adjective "contracted" as evidence of the "contract," the formal agreement, that God is initiating with future Christians like Herbert to designate Jesus as his intermediary. Whereas some readers will accept this second reading as a possibility, others will insist that this sense of "contracted" is too mundane to be juxtaposed with "glorious."

A third problem happens when someone chooses one of a variety of possible meanings that other interpreters claim does not fit other aspects of the utterance. For example, in this passage from the third poem of Adrienne Rich's "Twenty-One Love Poems," the final word could be interpreted in at least two different ways, but most would find only one of those meanings valid:

> Did I ever walk the morning streets at twenty,
> my limbs streaming with a purer joy?
> did I lean from any window over the city
> listening for the future
> as I listen here for nerves tuned for your ring? (26)

Because of the words "listening" and "listen," as well as the phrase, "nerves tuned," one will usually assume that the "ring" identified with the addressee is the sound of a telephone and not a gold or silver symbol of the lovers' commitment to one another. However, would a student be justified in "correcting" another member of the class who insists that both the auditory "ring" and the physical one demonstrate a richness of ambiguous signification? My imagined interpreter could assert that the speaker would "listen" intently "for" her beloved's expression of commitment, both a phone call and her bestowal of a circular piece of metal as token of the promise of a bond that extends into "the future." The other student then points out that one looks and does not listen for the bestowal of a physical token. The first student responds that "nerves tuned" is already a case of synesthesia connected with the anticipation (and perhaps anxiety) involving the "ring." Listening to this discussion, an instructor would feel that the second student's appeal to "realistic" context has common sense on its side. But when is the associative sprawl of poetry ever quite confined to common sense?

Finally, some of my students over the years have wielded a pre-established belief that a unit of language should yield a single meaning—that linguistic communication should always be transparent and there is an imperative to choose between differing meanings (and not affirm multiple ones). Seeing no contextual clues in the poem to lead to the "right" choice, such a student can become frustrated and angry. Resenting ambiguity, s/he will consider it a weakness of the text. But since many students are comfortable with ambiguity in punny jokes, movies, TV shows, song lyrics, etc., a professor can encourage everyone to apply the same tolerance for ambiguous poetic discourse.

Narrative (in)coherence is an especially significant marker of perceived accessibility/difficulty. In his lengthy, ambitious tome *Difficulty in Poetry: A Stylistic Model* (2019), Davide Castiglione states, "the more narrative a poem (i.e. the more it can be mapped onto a narrative schema), the more easily" that readers can understand it (153). However, he generalizes that "the narrativity of twentieth century poetry tends to appear in weakened forms when compared to most fictional writing," since narrative elements in modern and contemporary verse—and I'd add, *experimentally inclined* as opposed to traditional verse—are more often presented in fragmentary or "fractured" form than in earlier poetry. Problems are created by "shifts in time reference" or "shifts in place reference" (150) that are not clearly indicated, or by the "removal of" other important "connectives" (151) that would make the development of a series of actions clear.

A collage-oriented assembling of diverse narratives that lack a single, immediately discernible frame tends to challenge discernment of narrative coherence. Such a poem may seem to feature a single voice or resemble a gathering of diverse voices, but one that is not unified by the kind of dialogic structure found in traditional drama. Often, the voices are not named or given sufficient characterization. And they may not seem to be addressing each other directly. (T.S. Eliot's *The Waste Land* famously identifies voices/texts *only after* the poem has ended—in his notes, which, as Mary Karr notes, are not always useful.) Castiglione points to "register mixing" in relation to the absence of a single speaker, in which "linguistic choices associated with different speech situations and formality levels are bluntly juxtaposed or seamlessly merged"; in such cases "difficulty" occurs "only when each register variety resists being traced back to an identifiable speaker" (150).

But does a collage-poem's disruption of narrativity actually bother today's students? Hank Lazer, an innovative poet-critic, envisions "a typical student sitting … with an iPod plugged into one ear, listening to some music, holding a cell phone and reading a text message, while talking to the person across the table," etc., to show that today's "multitasking" millennial and post-millennial students are already acclimated to this kind of experience and are prepared for an open encounter with collage-poetry. Lazer speaks of our "over-determined world—one in which our verbal/linguistic comprehension occurs in a storm of language that cannot in any certain or conclusive manner yield to a unified understanding, much less a statement of the moment's 'theme'" (32). Ever since the advent of MTV music videos in the United States about four decades ago, popular versions of relatively disjunctive multimedia collage aesthetics have enjoyed a wide circulation.

Though many students accept and enjoy collage effects in other media than poetry, they don't have the responsibility to interpret these cultural products but can just experience whatever entertaining *frissons* are available and then dash to other experiences. (I'll return to this point later in the chapter in a discussion of Tan Lin's theory of ambient reading.) In an academic context, most college and university students understand that they are expected to perform fairly elaborate interpretation that supports a main point and thus dissociate this task from aesthetically based leisure, so they consistently look for a coherent narrative in poems (and literature in general). Therefore, dealing with collage-poems that resist the kind of analysis they are used to performing can give them a headache. Just as importantly, students who crave the pleasures of coherent narrative may expect it from literature and are irritated when they don't find it. Further, some students are so resistant to a poem's lack of narration that they stubbornly *ignore* the disjunctive or collagistic aspects and *impose* a coherent narrative—often one that covers a rather small part of the text.

Eileen R. Tabios's 1998 prose-poem "Come Knocking," which was published in her first two collections of poetry, is an example of a text with narrative elements that many readers would say do not cohere. In the last twenty years, Tabios has had no hesitation about articulating her conscious intentions, including the disruption of narrative, in numerous interviews and statements about her work. She stresses both the significance of these intentions and the importance of the reader's subjectivity going beyond them. In a 2007 interview with Tom Beckett, Tabios, who emigrated with her family from the Philippines to the United States when she was ten, discusses the influence of abstract visual art and her sociopolitical subject position on her decision to forego much narrative scaffolding in her work during the period "Come Knocking" was written:

> Abstraction is a key influence because of how it leaves open the interpretation of the image, in the same way that I write poems where meanings can't be fixed … As a Filipino poet who writes in English, I like to write poems where I am not communicating something

specific because the spread of English as a communications tool in the Philippines was one means through which the United States solidified its colonial rule of the Philippines in the 20th century.

(94)

While many of the Language poets in the seventies and eighties associate derailing of traditional narrative with the aim of exposing and countering "realism," "the illusion of reality in capitalist thought" (Silliman 10) that manipulates "the serialized-language consumer" (13), Tabios speaks of a specific postcolonial context for what seems a programmatic intention. (She prefers the term "transcolonial" to show that determinism stemming from the colonial past is not all pervasive.) The poet aligns this strategy of deleting clues about narrative specifics with the "notion of giving up authorial control" and sees it, "metaphorically, to be the opposite of colonialism" (Beckett Interview 94–95). In a 2014 interview with John Bloomberg-Rissman, Tabios speaks of her attempts "to disrupt notions of authorship as well as the conventionality of language through … abstraction, randomness, cubism, music, erasures, etc. Linear narrative comes up short for my poetry since it is contextualized within a world that contains results not derived from linear progressions. Certainly, justice does not unfold linearly, if it even unfolds" (31).

Like Charles Bernstein, whom I cited earlier, Tabios is not "killing" the author but removing support for the "notion of authorship" as the imposition of narrative coherence on readers. This imposition, she asserts, would falsely represent the complexity of actual events. Her programmatic intention is meant to free readers who would otherwise grant "obedience" to the idea that they must seek her active and final intentions to discover the text's "true" meaning. Nevertheless, I will try to show that attention to external evidence based on Tabios's stated allusions about her influences can help a reader develop conjectures that provide contexts for passages in "Come Knocking" where there might not seem to be any contexts. This will *not* enable readers to "fill in the blanks" and construct a relatively coherent narrative, but it will reduce the degree of opacity that they are likely to find in the text.

This prose-poem seems to have a single speaker and an addressee who might be involved or approaching/avoiding romantic involvement with the speaker. In various sentences, some contextual aspect of the two characters' interaction and possible conflict seems to be withheld, and the third paragraph focuses on the speaker alone in a different setting, while the fourth and final paragraph is filled with quasi-philosophical questions and a final address to the "you." One sometimes finds what Castiglione calls "removal of ... connectives" between one sentence and the next. Aspects of narrative incoherence are also frequently the result of other elements of difficulty discussed in this chapter, such as ambiguity, other tropes, and (possible) allusion. Though neither of Tabios's two characters is decisively identified by gender, I will assume that the speaker is a woman and the addressee is a man, as I am aware that many similar texts by this poet explicitly register female/male interactions. In a classroom situation, I would be explicit about my (imperfect) reason for how I construe gender, and I'd say that I'm doing it to avoid convoluted ways of talking about the characters. Here is the first paragraph:

> You quirked an eyebrow when I said I loved the flag. What else can be summoned when you have never seen me drop a smile? Then you admired the cherries hanging from the ears of a lady behind me. But as I turned my back I felt you raise your hand before it sadly lapsed. (26)

Without background information, it is unclear whether the speaker's opening declaration of affection is a sign of patriotism, an ironic swipe at it, or an aesthetic judgment that has nothing to do with politics. The object of "love" could be the red, white, and blue of the US flag, the red, white, blue, and yellow of the Philippine flag, or just a flag that the two characters happen to see. However, Tabios states in an interview with Purvi Shah that this text "was written partly in appreciation of one of Jasper Johns' works, 'Flag' (encaustic and collage on canvas, 1955) ..." (150). The word "encaustic" can be found in the second paragraph. "Come Knocking" appears for the second time in Tabios's collection,

Reproductions of the Empty Flagpole. Another poem in the book, "The Empty Flagpole," has an epigraph from poet/art critic John Yau's book, *The United States of Jasper Johns*: "The shifting relationship between the senses and the intelligence makes the apprehension of reality problematic, even when one repeatedly refuses, as [Jasper] Johns does, to succumb for the desire for asylum" (47). Yau develops an argument informed by his analysis of the artist's notorious paintings of the American flag, visible beneath an encaustic surface and above scraps of newspaper. In Yau's reading of the work, the paintings confound the questionable desire for purity—most notably, social unity through nationalism—with a critically powerful, complicated impurity.

I find it especially useful to apply external evidence to this first paragraph, because ambiguities make it hard for a reader to understand the two characters' motivation. The verb "drop" linked with the noun "smile" exemplifies the kind of ambiguity that pits opposites against each other: either the speaker "never" presents "a smile" or never gets rid of one that is already there. The smile could mean sincere pleasure, mockery, or ambivalence about her initial statement. So one cannot tell why the "you" must respond with a "quirked … eyebrow." And at the end of the paragraph, is a reader to assume that the addressee's "(col) lapsed" hand gesture expresses an intention of violence, tenderness, questioning, or a confusion between conscious and unconscious impulses? If one reads "the flag" as a reference to Yau's concepts about Johns's questioning of American nationalism during the mid-fifties and connects it with Tablos's statements about her motivation to perform transcolonial critique of the role of the United States in the Philippines's history, then the addressee's eyebrow motion following his seemingly rude shift of attention to another woman can be identified as his discomfort with the speaker's ideological perspective. Further, the raised hand (which responds to her physical answer to his change of focus) can be seen as a gesture of objection and an impulse to silence her. The gesture is withdrawn when the addressee realizes that it is rude, to say the least.

The second paragraph of the prose-poem begins with the man's attempt to evade an exploration of why the speaker "loves the flag":

> Someday we will discuss, you promised. It makes me order a
> drink. I know you admire encaustic for protecting forever the
> fragility of paper. But my friends begrudge you. Your blue
> shadows repel them. And they weep as I dive into the deep end. (26)

Although I think that the speaker's desire for a drink comically signifies her anxiety that the deferred discussion will *never* happen, the next sentence involving admiration for the material that protects the newsprint and paint on Johns's "Flag" canvas is attributed to the addressee. This is odd, because I'm provisionally assuming that he is supposed to be bothered by the painting's critique of nationalism, and not her. Is the speaker trying to display empathic understanding of the addressee by suggesting that, even if he doesn't like ideological implications of Johns's work, he appreciates the protective properties of "encaustic"? Perhaps it appeals to him because it is comparable to the gruff exterior he deploys to protect his own fragility against the "threat" of intimacy with her? Immediately, the introduction of new characters who disapprove of the addressee (and are not heard from again) discourages rapprochement, yet the final image, a romantic cliché of surrender, seems to indicate that the speaker does not listen to her friends and is surrendering to romance with the emotionally elusive "you."

Tantalizingly, the third paragraph's mini-narrative is disconnected from that amorous "deep end" and from the narrative content of the paragraphs that preceded it:

> I once rode an elephant through a field of tall grass. I laughed at
> a bear baring its yellow teeth. My guide was a pygmy who called
> me "Sir." My arms grew wiry tugging at rope. That evening,
> welts rose on my palms and I soothed them with the wet walls of
> a beer bottle. (26)

If this paragraph were detachable from the rest of the text, it would pose no difficulties for narrative comprehension. The only strange language is the substitution of the adjective "wiry" for the expected "weary," as it conveys the idea that musculature can change so quickly, as well as the concept that a bottle has "walls." While the second paragraph is set in a bar or restaurant, the setting here seems to be a jungle or nature preserve. The speaker is behaving as a tourist who exhibits power in the situation over the "guide" through the appellation "pygmy" and the mention of being addressed as "Sir." She feels secure enough to laugh at "a bear baring ... teeth." Yet the "welts" indicate that the speaker, despite her seemingly superior position, is not in control in this alien environment. She must be soothed by something familiar—not by ordering a drink, as in the second paragraph, but by using the moisture and coolness of a drink's container.

The portrayal of the speaker as nominally dominant *and* vulnerable in this environment may indicate how social positionality is not fixed but can fluctuate when conditions and contexts change. The collage-like juxtaposition of this brief narrative with the more elusive ones in the first two paragraphs could suggest that the third paragraph's complication of notions of social position informs the power dynamics between the speaker and her addressee. Either could have the upper hand at a given point. The speaker could use her critical consciousness to resist domination as much as she could "dive into the deep end."

The final paragraph of the prose-poem, which lacks a final period, balances three questions and three statements, none of which "advances" a "plot." Once again, the "you" is directly addressed, if it is the same "you":

> What is the surface of reality? Do not our fathers matter? Life so
> transcends one's intention. With what are we grappling when we
> are not sleeping? Why need we grapple when we are dreaming?
> How difficult it must be for you. And still, I must come knocking. (26)

The preposition "of" in the first question is ambiguous: does "reality" possesses a particular "surface" that is as "real" as "depth" or is the surface a superficial covering, while "reality" only exists in a depth? The speaker could be questioning whether the "surface" imagery in the first three paragraphs is part of some "reality" or obscuring one with simulacra. As for the question about paternal influence and inheritance, the assertion about "life transcend[ing] ... intention" may indirectly answer it by suggesting that "our fathers" (not mentioned earlier) "matter" so much that, in the course of "life," determinism seriously limits our free will. If a reader chooses to rely on external evidence about Tabios's transcolonial perspective and the influence of Yau's reading of Johns's flag painting, "fathers" can evoke "fatherlands," whose emblems include national flags. The question might be rhetorical, and glowing characterizations of nationalist pride, like father figures, "matter" too much, become too influential. The questions about difficulties of conscious experience and the reason for difficulties, such as nightmares, in unconscious processes continue to reflect the obstacles to fulfilling "one's intention." Recognizing the apparent pervasiveness of these individual existential challenges, the speaker expresses empathy for the addressee; compassion fuels her determination to muster the patience to continue to work toward achieving communication, despite his deferrals and/or evasions.

The prose-poem's title is echoed in its last two words, but one should not take the ringing aura of narrative closure too seriously. Even though small narrative progressions are recognizable, it takes a great deal of intricate guesswork and uncertain marshaling of external evidence to make a case for the idea that this text has any single narrative thread.

Vocabulary (whether abstract or concrete) that appears arcane to many readers can be a barrier to students' engagement with a poem. According to Castiglione, "specialised vocabulary greatly enhances [a reader's] sense of resistance," as it "slow[s] down or imped[es] decoding (lexical recognition and semantic access), which results in a more fragmentary or roughly sketched out situation model" and puts "disclosure of the poem's significance" (116) in jeopardy. If readers have to use a dictionary repeatedly to overcome this obstacle of a poem's abstruse language (and non-colloquial diction), they might lose patience with the interpretive process. But if they persevere, they will have the opportunity to gain appreciation for the play of language in imaginative poets like Gwendolyn Brooks, Forrest Gander (whose training in geology has permeated his poems), Marianne Moore, John Peck, and Wallace Stevens.

Relatively few poets utilize neologisms—what Castiglione cites as a subset of "morphological deviation" (107, 109, 110). Examples in English include e.e. cummings, Gerard Manley Hopkins, Lewis Carroll (in "Jabberwocky"), José Garcia Villa, and Bruce Andrews. James Joyce's novel *Finnegans Wake* has an abundance of neologisms on every page. In Tabios's "Come Knocking," the transformation of the adjective "quirky" to a verb "quirked" ("You quirked an eyebrow") might be considered a neologism. If a web search can't yield a definition of such coinages, the professor can lead a fruitful guessing game.

Vocabulary in dialect poetry may frustrate students, but it also provides a chance to enjoy the tension between a word or phrase in dialect and the corresponding one in "standard English," whether it's a matter of spelling or a more substantial transformation. When I teach poems by the Jamaican national heroine Louise Bennett, students—with the help of a class member whose family stems from Jamaica, in the best circumstances—tend to be patient enough to work through challenges of "translation." They often reach an admiration for the poet's biting ironies and her subversive use of what Kamau Brathwaite calls "Nation Language" in quatrains with frequent iambic meter and *rime croisée*. In the much-anthologized poem "Colonization in Reverse," the difficulty (and fascination) of Bennett's idiomatic English involves an intersection of vocabulary/spelling with grammar/syntax. Students don't take long to grasp why the Jamaican idiom is an especially apt form in which to communicate enduring effects of Britain's long-term colonial expropriation of wealth and labor from Jamaica through a pseudo-reversal. Idiomatic phrasing energetically delivers the irony of the "tunabout"—a compound noun in which "turn" and (change of) "tune" can be heard—that Bennett pretends is impoverishing "English people," and the poem pokes fun at "loyalty" to a travel agency that actually reduces the human resources of Jamaica.

To emphasize their particular source of difficulty, S.R. Levin and Davide Castilgione refer to unusual combinations of words as "semantic deviance" (Castigilione 130). This category includes tropes such as metaphor, simile, metonymy, and synecdoche. Since many prize fresh tropes as evidence of imagination, I'd prefer to call this **semantic deviation** in lieu of the pejorative *deviance*.

The major difficulty that readers face when encountering metaphor is figuring out how the vehicle fits the tenor, as the pair are often called in literary critical discourse, or, in linguistics, how the source domain fits the target domain. (In a literature class, I usually dispense with such terms and simply refer to the interaction between the main item being described and the item used to describe it and later, for economy's sake, refer to the former as A, the later as B, and the interpreted connection(s) between the two as C.) When class discussion reaches a specific metaphor, I find it better to elicit students' thoughts about what points of comparison are at play and help them elaborate on them than to present my own analysis, but I also find it useful to point out regularities in how metaphors tend to "behave."

In their 1980 book *Metaphors We Live By*, linguist George Lakoff and philosopher Mark Johnson provide three overlapping categories based on particular characteristics of the "entailments" (what I call "connections") between a target domain and a source domain. These categories can assist students in becoming more comfortable with the analysis of metaphor and simile. Their book seems best known for the distinction between "conventional metaphors," which, they argue, have tremendous (yet often hidden) explanatory power in a given culture, and "novel" or "new metaphors" (128–129), which "highlight things not usually highlighted by our normal conceptual structure" (180), often appear in poetry, and can sometimes eventually become "conventional" and highly influential. But the three categories apply to both conventional and novel metaphors.

The first of Lakoff and Johnson's categories of metaphor is "structural": "cases where one concept is metaphorically structured in terms of another" (15). Here, "one highly structured and clearly delineated concept" is employed "to structure another" (61), but the structuring is partial, since "it can be extended in some ways but not others" (14). In her praise-poem "Langston Hughes," Gwendolyn Brooks utilizes numerous structural metaphors to describe Hughes's impact on African-Americans:

Holds horticulture
In the eye of the vulture
Infirm profession.
In the Compression—
In mud and blood and sudden death—
In the breath
Of the Holocaust he
Is helmsman, hatchet, headlight. (123)

To keep my illustration of structural metaphor concise, I will only discuss five metaphors out of the eleven or twelve tropes in these eight lines. In all cases, the tenor is not stated; the allusion to Langston Hughes in the title and some external evidence about his place in US history, including the Harlem Renaissance, can fill in these gaps. Without external evidence, speculation would be aimless.

"Horticulture" is a metaphor in which the process and effects of garden cultivation bear comparison with those of Hughes's aesthetic and ideological nurturing of African-Americans, who are beleaguered by perpetrators of racism. Racists and institutional racism are signified by the metaphor of the "vulture," further complicated by its inclusion in the trope substituting "the eye of the vulture" for "the eye of the hurricane" which depends on their mutual evocation of violence. In the trio of alliterative nouns in the passage's last line, note the contrast between "helmsman"/"headlight" and "hatchet." "Helmsman" and "headlight" emphasize Hughes's activities and functions in his people's uplift through aesthetic/intellectual, ideological, and psychological leadership and teaching respectively, whereas "hatchet" focuses on his efforts and status as a critic of "the vulture" and "the Holocaust." In an interview, when Etherbert Miller asks Brooks why she characterizes Hughes as a "hatchet," she responds that this "shouldn't need any explanation," because the poet was "going out into our world and hacking away at things he thought were wrong" (104). The metaphors depend on the correlation between the structure of racist practices, the resistance to those practices, and the general empowerment of African-Americans with the structures of functions and desired effects associated with the particular vehicles. A careful breakdown of the structural features of such entailments, perhaps with diagrams, can help perplexed students.

Lakoff and Johnson's second category concerns "*orientational metaphors*," which mostly entail "spatial orientations," "aris[ing] from the fact that we have bodies ... and that they function as they do in our physical environment" (15). Using either "spatial metaphor" or "metaphor of location" might make the concept easier for students to assimilate. During our cyber era, technological advances have called into question previous notions of spatial and temporal proximity. Geoffrey Young's 2016 unrhymed sonnet, "The Way We Are," displays orientational metaphors to comment wryly on this phenomenon. Here is the second half of the poem:

The post-modern condition has delivered us well beyond

the reach of the Apocalypse. We are camped out
in the utopia of digital immortality, on intimate terms
with that which obliterates each grotesque feeling of distance
we might find in ourselves, powered

by techno-wonders that sweep away life's pains
in scintillating waves of intense electrified connection. (5)

The metaphor of "beyond/ the reach" to indicate "our" protection from "the Apocalypse" functions because of a correlation between a set of concepts ("the post-modern condition") creating or facilitating a mental state (that's "far" from a traditional Christian's fear of ultimate judgment) and the influence of a mode of transportation on someone's physical distance from a spatial location. Similarly, "the utopia of digital immortality" is not an actual place but a psychological tendency that *feels* like an entertaining, spacious physical place where "we" are able to "locate" ourselves ("camp out"). Although a computer or smart phone is literally in one's environment, and one is not literally *inside* the object that s/he manipulates and obtains sensory images from, the metaphor can convey the spatial illusion as a seemingly genuine, "intimate" experience. The next orientational metaphor translates the abstract sense of cognitive/affective dissonance or "grotesque" alienation in one's thoughts/feelings from one's other thoughts into an image of spatial self-division. (There is no literal "feeling of distance"; metaphor yokes "feeling" and "distance" together.) I read the speaker as having an ironic perspective on this "condition"; the negative metaphorical construct, abetted by how enjambments create *separations* and "distance" rather than "intimate terms," has much more rhetorical force than the assertion that cybertechnology can "obliterate" this and similar kinds of "life's pains" with a dubious "connection."

The third of Lakoff and Johnson's categories is *"ontological metaphors,"* which provide "ways of viewing events, activities, emotions, ideas, etc. as entities and substances" (26); "events and actions are conceptualized metaphorically as objects, activities as substances, states as containers" (31). Philosophy majors will have no trouble with this locution, but the professor can refer to the category as "metaphor of being" for other class members' benefit. These metaphors serve in the act of "referring," "quantifying," "identifying aspects," "identifying causes," and "setting goals and motivating actions" (26–27). In "Presence," Rosario Castellanos, one of Mexico's most influential twentieth-century feminist poets, finds various ontological metaphors for bodily existence and later, one for the speaker's identity composed of diverse experiences of intense emotion:

One day I will know it. This body that has been
my shelter, my prison, my hospital, is my tomb ... .

This knot that I was (of furies,
betrayals, hopes,
sudden glimpses, desertions,
hungers, cries of fear and helplessness
and happiness shining in the darkness
and words of love and love and loves)
will be cut by the years.

In the opening lines of Victoria Cox's translation, the notion of a container is the metaphorical correlation between the body (tenor) and of the four vehicles. The tenor contains the mind or soul of the person, and the first three vehicles contain the body and mind, while the last contains only the remains. The ontological metaphors identify features of the body's interaction with and subjection to its environment, whether physical or social. "Shelter" indicates the living body's positive, protective functions, "prison" indicates circumstances in which containment in a body is oppressive (perhaps referring to patriarchal constraints on women), and "hospital" connotes both illness and the potential for recovery, so the last vehicle "tomb"—turning a body into a corpse—has a potent finality that signifies ontological limits.

The connection between "this knot" and the numerous references to emotions and gestures in the parentheses entails the effect of a complex process of formation. This ontological metaphor includes both "identifying aspects" and "identifying causes" as an image of physical "knotting" is seen to resemble an accretion of psychological complications. The further expansion of the metaphor with "cutting" (which operates along with the metonymy of "years") does suggest that ontological complexity is eliminated and replaced by "simplicity" but that, ironically, as in the body/tomb connection, this violent action severs the "string" or "rope" of life itself.

Lakoff and Johnson consider instances of personification "the most obvious ontological metaphors" (34), as they permit users "to make sense of phenomena in the world in human terms—terms that we can understand on the basis of our own motivations, goals, actions, and characteristics" (35). I would surmise that in "This Poem," Beckett uses personification with great rhetorical awareness and with the active intention of posing problems, not achieving fixed statements, about ontology and epistemology. Thus, his use of the trope doesn't qualify as conventional ontological metaphor.

Lakoff and Johnson hold that metaphors, even ones with a long string of entailments, have limited applicability and offer partial comprehension of a phenomenon. Even though metaphor is an extremely important means of seeking partial comprehension of "our feelings, aesthetic experiences, moral practices, and spiritual awareness" (194), which elude full understanding, Lakoff and Johnson acknowledge that its "systematicity that allows us to comprehend one aspect of a concept in terms of another ... will necessarily hide other aspects of the concept" and prevent "us from focusing on [those] aspects that are inconsistent with the metaphor" (11). On the other hand, a reader might be fixated exclusively on attributes of the target domain of a metaphor or simile that have nothing to do with those of the source domain, so that s/he does not find entailments that others do and therefore will not find meaning in the trope.

Scholars who think theoretically about tropes routinely invoke Roman Jakobson's pronouncements about metaphor and metonymy: "The development of a discourse may take place along two different semantic lines: either through their similarity or through their contiguity" (1152). Jakobson speaks of "the *metaphoric way*," which involves a combination of elements, as pertaining to similarity and "the *metonymic* way," which involves selection, in relation to contiguity. In his alignment of metaphor with condensation and metonymy with displacement, Jacques Lacan utilizes Jakobson's formulation to articulate the resemblance between Freud's theory of the workings of the unconscious and the operations of language. (See *Écrits*, 421–431.) Some theorists subsume synecdoche under the category of metonymy, but I think that it's valuable to identify them separately. In poetry, one can read language representing parts of the body and the voice as a synecdoche for the individual as a whole entity or, at times, a divided self.

In her poem, "Good Mirrors Are Not Cheap" Audre Lorde makes an interesting use of synecdoche and a critique of a certain kind of metonymy when her speaker asserts that "hating a mirror/ or its reflection" is a wasteful activity and that instead, one should stop "the hand/ that makes glass with distortions ..." (67). Because people literally use their hands to create mirrors, the poet through synecdoche selects the hand to stand in place of the actual perpetrator of "distortions."

Hatred comprises a metonymic displacement of a cause to its effect. The speaker finds it useless to blame the object of representation and the depiction itself (the effect). She believes that one should take action against the producer of such objects (cause) to prevent further situations in which "the fault in a mirror" creates "error." What complicates the reading of tropes in this poem is how the "mirror" acts as a metaphor, a concrete image for any kind of representation—whether spoken, printed, televised, etc.—of one person or group by another. However, the metaphor itself is reasonably common, and both the synecdoche and metonym are traceable to the concept of agency on the part of the one who faces the mirror and its maker.

After citing many writers who have tried to pin down metonymy, Hugh Bredin cogently defines it as "a transfer of names between objects which are related to one another extrinsically and simply" (57). Rather than emphasizing selection, he asserts that "its role in language and in thought is that it articulates the enterprise of combining our objects of thought into larger wholes." By calling the relations of the two elements of metonyms "extrinsic," Bredin means that they "are relations among things" rather than "within things" (53), as in synecdoche. And metonymy features "a simple relation" because it does not include the dependence of one object on the other (55), as synecdoche does. Bredin observes that since "a metonymy neither states nor implies the connection between the objects involved in it," "we must *already know* that the objects are related, if the metonymy is to be devised or understood"; therefore, it "can never articulate a newly discovered insight" but it "is ... necessarily conventional" (58).

David Reid strongly disagrees with Bredin that metonymy cannot produce imaginative effects. Despite how it "typically plays on ready-made associations" (918), Reid claims that "all well-turned metonymy makes play of its way of upsetting the natural order of things" in order "to surprise and disturb our conventional" perceptions; "it plays with irrationality only to intimate a rational thought between the lines" (922). Reid finds both "reductive" and "visionary" or "surrealistic" possibilities in metonymy (920). These "reductive" possibilities might be called "dead metonymy," since many widely circulating examples of metonymy are so familiar that their metonymic properties have been forgotten and they seem "literal" to those who use them. Whether one agrees with Reid or Bredin depends on reader-response: if a relation between the two elements is something that the reader would not ordinarily consider and thus finds striking, it is unimportant that s/he might already "know" it. Sudden recognition differs from humdrum recognition, so the disagreement can only be settled on a case-by-case basis with particular readers.

In instances where Reid proves right, the effects of imaginative transformation of perception engendered by metonymy—as well as metaphor and simile—might prompt students who cherish direct statement to be suspicious of it, rather than gain pleasure from it. They might fixate on the literal sense of the word or phrase that is metonymically displacing a referent rather than seeing that they should trace the trope back to the referent. Or they might not grasp how contiguity between elements produces meaning in a particular phrase, clause, or sentence. When this happens, if a professor makes use of Hugh Bredin's list of eleven "metonymic relations" (without necessarily "teaching" the whole list to a class), then s/he can help students grasp relations more easily; the list includes: "cause/effect," "inventor/invented, "user/instrument," "doer/thing done," "passion/object of passion," "container/contained," "place/object in place," "time/object in time," "possessor/possessed," "sign/signified," "concrete/abstract" (48). (In my view, the last category could confuse some issues for students, since so many metaphors exhibit an abstract tenor and a concrete vehicle.)

Poland's Nobel laureate Wisława Szymborska's poem "Museum" not only consists mostly of metonyms but features metonymy a major aspect of its subject matter:

> Here are plates but no appetite.
> And wedding rings, but the requited love
> has been gone now for some three hundred years.

Here's a fan—where is the maiden's blush?
Here are swords—where is the ire?
Nor will the lute sound at the twilight hour.

Since eternity was out of stock,
ten thousand aging things have been amassed instead. (30)

In the metonymic economy of a historical museum display, the speaker finds that possessions are associated with their possessors ("plates," "rings," "fan"), users with their instruments ("swords," "lute"), and signs with their signifieds ("rings"). Yet the gap between the present and the lives of those owners and users teaches her that this physical "performance" of metonymy manifests the absence of the owners' and users' lives. The display presents objects that no longer fulfill the function for which they were created and no longer benefit those individuals in the way that they were intended to do. "Eternity" is always "out of stock," because metonymy cannot reestablish the presence of the human beings associated with the objects. Personification contributes to the effect; former possessions, instruments, and signs, however currently "useless," "survive" the late former possessors:

The crown has outlasted the head.
The hand has lost out to the glove.
The right shoe has defeated the foot.

As for me, I am still alive, you see.
The battle with my dress still rages on.
It struggles, foolish thing, so stubbornly!
Determined to keep living when I'm gone! (30)

The mortal speaker—including the author of "Museum" who died in 2012—knows that her ability to enjoy ownership and use is finite, that the same situation of the original possessors of the museum's objects will eventually befall her. Regarding the different perspectives of Reid and Bredin on the imaginative potential of metonymy, "Museum" causes me to reflect upon the implications of historical museum displays in a way that I did not consider before reading the poem, so in this case, I side with Reid.

Irregularities of syntax—what Davide Castiglione, following S. R. Levin, terms "syntactic deviance" (140)—are often sources of difficulty. I will call it **syntactic deviation**. Castiglione notes the challenges of "syntactic complexity" (141–142), "syntactic ambiguity," in which "a structure enables two distinct parsing routes and results in two different ideational representations" and thus makes "demands ... both on parsing and on the construction of meaning" (140), and "phrase-based syntax," which "halts before the clause rather than overstepping it," in order to pursue "fragmentation," resulting in "information deficit" (142–143). "Phrase-based syntax" requires "cues ... 'from outside', through pragmatic inferencing" (143).

The title of Paolo Javier's poem "Feeling Its Actual" slightly deviates from *The Feeling Is Actual*, the title of the 2011 book in which it appears. When the book was published, Javier, who is originally from the Philippines, was serving as Poet Laureate of his current home borough, Queens, New York, one of the United States' most ethnically and racially diverse areas. In "Feeling Its Actual," the unnamed female speaker's lack of control over idiomatically and syntactically standard English can create problems for readers involving syntactic deviation, but those readers may also discover imaginative constructions of meaning. Ambiguity begins with the title. The lack of an apostrophe in the second word could be an error of omission indicating "feeling that it is actual," with the pronoun "it" suggesting a host of referents, or it might also signify omission of punctuation between the first two words: "feeling—it's actual," an endorsement of emotional authenticity. But "its" might take a possessive form rather than being a contraction of a subject and copular verb; thus, there would be an omission if a noun were attached to the adjective "actual" at the end, or else the adjective may be intended to have the weight of the noun "actuality."

At the beginning of the poem the speaker focuses (in English) on the difficulty that she faces in negotiating with a new environment via a new tongue. She expresses frustration, some self-reproach for her "errors," and criticism of language's limitations:

> why did i always
> use the wrong words
> should be other words
> that are more suitable
> language is quite strange
> and make me so confused
> i often cannot understand
> what they say. (136)

The adjective "suitable" pictures English as a wardrobe that could be more versatile. The fifth line seems to say that *all* language has built-in limitations, yet the conjunction "and" in the next line, as well as the lack of understanding of "what they [native English speakers?] say" may suggest that the speaker has left out a word modifying "language." It's *this* language (English) which is odd to her. The subject/verb disagreement involving "language" and "make" suggests an area in which English grammar behaves arbitrarily; the parent language, unknown to us, might not. This arbitrary quality is intensified by the coordinating conjunction "and," which often reflects a plural subject, but here, a plural verb. "Language" is actually the co-presence of two (or more) languages in the speaker's mind. Conceptually, it is both a singular and plural subject at once, making for a "strangeness" that produces "confusion" about the verb ending. Coming directly after a correct usage of the same verb, another example of a third-person singular subject/verb disagreement is also illuminating:

> i want to hide in a place
> that makes me comfortable
> this sofa feels like
> the peafowls feathers
> very comfortable
> make me feel ecstatic. (136)

On the one hand, the nonstandard "make" in the last line might comprise the speaker's demand for comfort (that is not separated from prior syntactical units by a semi-colon, dash, or period). On the other hand, if we judge the verb as a grammar error, "ecstatic" emotion results from the speaker's strong association between the sensation of her current sofa and a cherished memory from her native land ("peafowls feathers") that permits her imagination to return home momentarily. In the last part of the next strophe, a verb form error, followed by the unconventional construal of a preposition, makes inventive use of the binaries imagination/reality and past/present:

in fact i just need to imagine
what i want or fancy what
will be happened
if i dont want something
to happen, i go away
i miss my home too
time can stop in anytime
for the weather is cold
all day long. (136)

Although "will be happened" indicates that the desired future—at least in "fancy"—is a repetition of the past, it is balanced by the speaker's expression of her homesickness and mention of her new environment's emotionally and physically "cold" "weather." "Going away" signifies ignoring an unpleasant current reality or departing from a situation (to the extent that she can); ironically, it echoes her family's act of leaving their homeland. Next, the placement of the little preposition "in" has a significant impact: "time can" *enter* ("stop in") to disrupt the eternal present/presence of nostalgic reverie "anytime" (doubling the reference to time in a single line), *or* it can *cease* ("stop") *at* any point to be itself. That is, sudden death ends life, even if the implication of death is itself a figure for exile as the end of a happy life. Therefore, depending on the significance or irrelevance that one attaches to the preposition, "time" is either a helpful or a threatening entity in the struggle to fulfill desire against whatever would negate it. In the next strophe, the line is repeated; it follows the statement, "time wont stop just for you" (137), which indicates that one cannot live in a marvelous eternal present. The speaker alternates between moments of resignation about difficult reality—"I can be this way concedingly"—and determination to fulfill wishes. Having the makeshift adverb "concedingly" modify the verb "can be" suggests that the speaker chooses to behave provisionally in response to a particular context rather than to succumb permanently to pessimism.

Small changes in syntax create confusion that can only be resolved by appeal to arbitrary idiomatic conventions: "i always cant be clear/ about all these things" (139). For a native English speaker, the fact that the adverb comes before the verb makes the immigrant speaker say that she *never* achieves clarity, even as common sense tells us that she admits that clarity can happen but not every time ("can't always"). But what logic justifies a native speaker's feeling that "always can't" sounds wrong, whereas "I can never be clear" is appropriate?

Sometimes, when readers tend to fill in syntactic gaps easily, these gaps signify in interesting ways. For example, after the speaker flirts with the concept, "We're all the same," she then disrupts the authority of a homogenizing "mirror" as translation becomes an issue: "if we face the mirror/ would become the same person/ its something about the light/ but i don't know what hes saying/ hes only got one eye" (139). In the second line, the deletion of the independent clause's subject (the "we" that does not get reiterated but disappears) in effect "makes" more than one person into a single individual ("the same" in "the mirror"). As for the encounter with a one-eyed man, the limitation of vision is associated with a limited (monolingual?) ability to communicate.

Describing her mother's influence near the poem's end, the speaker declares: "i was following her footsteps/ and i am too determined/ to make my way alone" (140). Omission of the preposition "in" does not affect the speaker's ability to convey how she follows her mother's attitude, but I read the substitution of "too" for the expected "very" both as an admirable expression of intense determination and as a potential problem if the speaker overlooks the need for interdependence in a difficult environment. The misuse of the indefinite article in the sentence that follows displays a particular logic: "i was not a great cook but/ i have a great eyes for details" (140). "Eyes" are plural but work together as a single entity; the idiom "an eye for detail" implies the plural within the singular. The speaker preserves both components. The poem's final line appears on a new page to underscore the speaker's double awareness: "'Your pillow is outside itself'" (141). If this is a "pillow" of nostalgia for the homeland, it is "inside out," exposed to effects of present challenges and difficulties of accessing memory.

In treating the syntactical deviations of a poem like "Feeling Its Actual" in class discussion, I don't use as many grammatical terms as I just did. Protracted attention to grammar will bore, irritate, or sidetrack many students; instead, I focus on comparing possible rephrasings of passages to the original phrases and clauses.

Categorization (of a text as poetry or not) often reflects difficulties caused by a reader's beliefs, which shape their aversions and predilections. Although I have alluded to this kind of difficulty earlier in this chapter in connection with narrative (in)coherence and other concerns, it is sufficiently important to discuss as a separate category. George Steiner refers to this as "modal difficulty," and he defines it as an "atrophy of response whose autonomous force of life, whose *raison d'être* in the strict sense of the phrase, escapes us" (268). Insisting that modal difficulty is "not, or not only, a question of taste" (268), Steiner states that the reader finds the poem's articulation of "a stance toward human conditions ... essentially inaccessible or alien," and "the root-occasion of the poem's composition eludes or repels our internalized sense of what poetry should or should not be about, of what are the intelligible, morally and aesthetically acceptable moments and motives for poetry" (267). Reginald Shepherd refers to the inability to "determine what kind of poem" a text "is" as not knowing "how to read it, in much the same sense that one might try and fail to 'read' a person"; "this difficulty," he states, often manifests itself when "poems ... play with or violate conventions and expectations."

After hearing others say what a poem cannot include or consist of—a laundry list, a meteorological report, shopping items, a recipe, the transcription of a trial, travel directions, a computer algorithm, tabloid gossip—many poets put such "proscribed" items in verse. Marcel

Duchamp's exhibition of an actual urinal as sculpture is a dramatic example of an artwork that precipitated a storm of modal difficulty. He paved the way for pop art like Andy Warhol's Campbell soup paintings nearly half a century later and, arguably, what is now called Conceptual Writing/Poetry exemplified by such authors as Tan Lin, Kenneth Goldsmith, Vanessa Place, and Robert Fitterman. Goldsmith transcribed a year's worth of weather forecasts in his 2005 book, *The Weather*. In *Inbox*, Noah Eli Gordon appropriates, in reverse chronological order "the body-text of every email that was addressed specifically to [him]" on a given day so that he can "let all of the voices collide into one continuous text" (4). But can one read such a text as one reads *a poem*? Emphasizing how the emails in *Inbox* frequently address issues significant to Gordon's poetry community, Daniel Morris reads the book "as a mimesis with dialogical significance, and literary sociological import" (192).

On the other hand, Tan Lin supports a kind of "scanning" of category-bending poetic texts that challenges the primacy of textual interpretation. Lin envisions "lyricism, subjectivity, and personal expressiveness ... reduced to blips in an ambient sound track, where historical markers (of cultural products) could be erased, and where nonreading, relaxation, and boredom could be the essential components of a text"; he valorizes "poetry" that aspires "to the condition of variable moods, like relaxation and yoga and disco" ("Disco as Operating System," 96–7). In a 2009 response to a review of his book, *Plagiarism/Outsource* (Zasterle, 2008), also known in later editions as *Heath*, Lin acknowledges that "critical reading and rereading" of the kind that concerns us in this book "is useful as a practice, but it's a relatively narrow practice, like footnoting, that is commonly situated in academic or high literature settings: in other words, directed at work that is *meant* to be read and reread" ("A Response to Thomas Fink"). He wanted his book to reflect how "text production and reading have changed with recent text distribution practices" and have departed from "sustained, critical reading practices" toward an encounter with "'content' that is jointly produced or produced under socially networked conditions, content that is harder to classify as 'original' or pleasurable—as opposed to, say, boring." Lin explores "'social reading' on the periphery of one's attention …'"

The kinds of literary texts (hybrid texts that include literary elements) that Lin produces and champions probe boundaries that affect categorizations. When they are discussed in a college literature classroom, I presume that these theoretical elements need to be at the forefront; the texts are a jumping off point for thinking about larger sociological, economic, political, psychological, or philosophical issues and not an occasion for close reading. In this way, they differ from other poetry that defies the limits of prior categorizations yet still warrants close reading and not the cultivation of distraction.

While the history of art and poetry includes the record of a continually expanding sense of its thematic and formal possibilities, what seems to be a general consensus of a poetry community at any given time is not empirically verifiable. Different poetry (and academic) communities often disagree about what qualifies as poetry and what doesn't. We can imagine how Walt Whitman's use of free verse in *Song of Myself* vexed groups of mid-nineteenth-century partisans of traditional meter and rhyme, while it appealed to Emerson. As for readers unaffiliated with any particular literary group, such as many students in an introduction to literature class, they may have criteria forged by their specific cultural experiences.

Reviewing the components of the barriers to access and engagement that I've treated in this chapter and imagining how several can function with negative synergy in encounters with a text, I conclude that I need to become *more* understanding, *more* patient, *more* perseverant in helping students overcome each obstacle and increase their own patience and perseverance with poems. In "The Difficult Poem," a masterful parody of the discourse of self-help books that capitalizes on an extended analogy between poems and people, Charles Bernstein's earnest self-help poetry guru declares: "Don't let the poem intimidate you! Often the difficult poem will provoke you, but this may be its way of getting your attention. Sometimes, if you give your full attention to the poem, the provocative behavior will stop" (*Attack of the Difficult Poems* 5).

2

Emotional Enticements and Aversions

Regardless of how serious literature faculty are about teaching interpretation of poetry as "critical thinking," can they afford to forget that one of the prime rewards for reading poetry has to do with emotional experience? Let's go back a couple of millennia and ask Aristotle. In the *Poetics*, he argues that one of the "two causes" of the creation of poetry is "the instinct of imitation," which is "implanted in man [*sic*] from childhood, … and through imitation learns his earliest lessons; and no less universal is the pleasure felt in things imitated" (55). The creator takes pleasure in pursuing *mimesis* and transfers this enjoyment to his or her audience: "Objects which in themselves we view with pain, we delight to contemplate when reproduced with minute fidelity: such as the forms of the most ignoble animals and of dead bodies," because "to learn gives the liveliest pleasure"; when they contemplate "a likeness," people "find themselves learning or inferring, and saying perhaps, 'Ah, that is he.' For if you happen not to have seen the original, the pleasure will be due not to the imitation as such, but to the execution, the coloring, or some such other cause" (55–56).

Intimately bound with the concept of imitation in the *Poetics* is *catharsis*, which Aristotle applies to tragedy and uses in relation, specifically, to the emotions of fear and pity. (When it is applied to lyric poetry, the range of emotions naturally expands.) Aristotle does not define the term. Over the centuries, scholars have put forth differing interpretations of *catharsis*. One prominent view is that it is a "purging" of the emotions and hence a "purification" of one experiencing them. In his introduction to S. H. Butcher's translation of the *Poetics*, Francis Fergusson cites Aristotle's observation in the *Politics* that "in religious rituals that he knew, the passions were stirred, released, and at last appeased" and reasons that, for the philosopher, *catharsis* ("purgation") identifies tragedy's "effect [as] *like* that which believers get from religious ceremonies intended to cleanse the spirit" (35). Some scholars stress a cognitive component in the "cleansing" and others do not.

For audience members to experience catharsis while watching a play by August Wilson or William Shakespeare, reading a novel by Toni Morrison or Isabel Allende, or experiencing a Homeric epic, it would obviously require investment of a much more substantial amount of time than it would for a lyric poem. Stephanie Burt declares that lyric poems can masterfully embody "small models of complicated feelings," made "out of words and nothing else" and made to "last longer than any one moment or any one lifetime"; such admirably compact texts "do not just say how somebody feels … ; they show those feelings, giving them shape and sound" (5).

Though it is obvious that a reader's experience of identification with a poem's persona or lyric "I" (or a character that the speaker represents) frequently induces her to experience feelings communicated in that poem, "attachments to artworks are the result not of a single, all-powerful cause steering things behind the scenes but of different things coming together in ways that are often hard to pin down" (9), as Rita Felski argues in *Hooked: Art and Attachment*. Felski cites the notion of "distributed agency" in Bruno Latour's "Actor-network theory" to support this point. For her, the most prominent factors in forming a reader's identification with a character in a literary text are "alignment," the result of an author's deliberate emphases, the reader's "allegiance" to particular moral or political values, his/her "recognition" of parallels between his/her experience and that of the character, and "empathy" (xiii) with depicted emotions. Felski also includes "ironic identification" involving "shared dissociation."

Regarding direct identification, Cristina V. Bruns in *Why Literature* stresses the importance of immersive reading prior to literary analysis in academic situations. She finds that a literary text can be comparable to psychologist D.W. Winnicott's transitional "object that is both attuned to what resides within the self in order to give it expression or articulation and that also adds to what is there" (28). Bruns asserts: "Seeing or discovering something of ourselves in a literary work can come with a shock when the resulting insight is troubling or as a relief when we find that some part of ourselves is shared with another" (19). After working through such a shock, a reader is often able to convert it into beneficial insight.

Edwin Creely credits the power of imagery in poetry as a catalyst of emotional identification: "Particular images may have affinity with a person and can thus evoke a reflexive response as part of a developing hermeneutics of self" (121). Creely speaks of "a constant and evolving interpretive framing of self that resonates from the poetic moment of exchange between the reader and the poetic text, even if the text might create alienation or disaffection for a reader." Similarly, but with greater theoretical specificity, Charles Altieri in *The Particulars of Rapture: An Aesthetic of the Affects* argues that one should think "of emotions in adverbial rather than adjectival terms" (107–8). This signifies that "emotions become ... modifiers of how people act rather than states people enter"—that is, "attributes of attitudes being formed by agents in ways that modify desire and hence indirectly modify actions" (108). Due to the "concrete vividness" of what one does to express the emotion, providing "the locus of significance for the activity," "we adjust how we project identities—about our own emotions or about agents whom we observe. We are responding ... to who the person becomes as he or she manifests the working out of attitudes in relation to [the person's] world" (125–6). In order to address how "working out of [people's] attitudes" functions adverbially, Altieri takes from Baruch Spinoza the notion of conative energy or force, which involves an individual's ability through adjustments to continue existing and behaving in ways that move toward greater satisfaction: "Identification is not just naming a process one's own. It is also testing how conative energies can be maintained and extended when we bring second-order considerations to bear on the spaces opened by our manners of acting" (144).

In her treatment of affect in literature, Eve Kosofsky Sedgwick puts forth the concept of "reparative reading," which she considers especially valuable for Queer Theory. Perhaps the idea has much in common with Horace's principle of "*dulce et utile*" (sweet and useful) as a powerful rationale for the value of literature and probably long before his time, but it has received substantially more attention in academe during the first two decades of this century than it did in the last two of the previous one.

Reparative reading never went into hibernation. Mark C. Jerng states that "from the inception of race and ethnic literary studies," critics have approached the reading of texts by "build[ing] forms of continuity, new interactions, and new connections in a self-reflexive way" as they have needed to construct "traditions otherwise devalued or rendered invisible" and, therefore, frequently focus on "drawing connections and ways of reading that valorize the political, social, and literary expressive possibilities" (267). In an article on the poetry of Thylias Moss, Ryan Cull notes how "praise poetry" practiced by "African American poets since Philis Wheatley" manages "to incite the consent of others, generating a discursive basis for community while also manifesting energies capable of promoting social change" (125). Cull goes as far as to declare that numerous African-American poets' mobilization of "this political potential within praise, mastering the delicate task of admiring while also critiquing aspects of American culture" has had, "as an affective register," an influence just as significant as "the blues in African American poetry." The representation of the strength and resilience of individuals in the face of sociopolitical oppression has been a central source of readers' positive identifications in literary texts by members of marginalized groups, as well as their critics' focus.

The 1997 essay in which Sedgwick first utilizes the term "reparative reading" relies on Melanie Klein's psychoanalytic theory regarding the paranoid and depressive positions and contrasts her viewpoint with Freud's. Klein characterizes "the depressive position" as "an anxiety-mitigating achievement that the infant or adult only sometimes, and often only briefly succeeds in inhabiting," the practice of using "one's own resources to assemble or 'repair' murderous part-objects into something like a whole—though, [Sedgwick] would emphasize, *not necessarily like any preexisting whole*" (128). Sedgwick presents camp as a reparative queer practice that has too often been exclusively associated with negative critique of hegemonic gender arrangements (150).

Gila Ashtor describes Sedgwick as breaking with "'sociological' interpretations that subsume individual psychology into culture or ideology by treating the individual as (merely) emblematic, or symptomatic, of material conditions" and instead "us[ing] the social conditions of literary texts to illuminate the pathways that desire can take ..." (209). Sedgwick, according to Ashtor, engages in "'speculative' analysis [which] problematizes the 'individual *as* a system,' where that system can be understood to be sexual, psychological, interpersonal, emotional, or technological" (195). While admitting that "gender reifications" could conceivably affect any "topic or area of psychoanalytic thought," Sedgwick rejects "an anticipatory mimetic strategy whereby" critics automatically assume (or impose) "a certain, stylized violence of sexual differentiation" because "it can never be finally *ruled out*" and because they feel the need to avoid horrible surprises (Sedgwick 132–133). Utilizing Silvan Tomkins's affect theory, Sedgwick worries that "the mushrooming, self-confirming strength" of such an anticipatory strategy will undermine "the ... goal of seeking positive affect" (136), including recognition of positive surprises (146). Tremendous suffering without avenues of reparation, she avers, does not facilitate development of strategies for the achievement of desired social change (144).

Sedgwick invokes the late phase of Michel Foucault's work, "the care of the self," as connected to the goal that both Klein and Tomkins foreground: "to provide the self with pleasure and nourishment in an environment that is perceived as not particularly offering them" (137). For her, "hope," which "is among the energies by which the reparatively positioned reader tries to organize the fragments and part-objects she encounters or creates" (146), is not to be dismissed. She calls "the reparative reading position" "no less realistic" and "attached to a project of survival" "than a paranoid position" (a hermeneutics of suspicion) in undertaking "a different range of affects, ambitions, and risks" (150). Sedgwick maintains that such reading provides understanding of "the many ways selves and communities succeed in extracting sustenance from the objects of a culture," even one hostile to their interests (150–151).

A perusal of the 2005 "Egg Rolls" by Denise Duhamel should illustrate how various concepts about affect that I have been discussing can be seen as playing out in a narrative poem. The speaker is a working-class graduate student at an elite institution, Sarah Lawrence, where Duhamel herself received her MFA. In the long opening strophe, after detailing minutely what she is forced to think about and endure, the speaker approaches shame about the idea that she could become a privileged person's object of pity:

> I was walking down First Avenue and knew
> my check wouldn't clear for another two days and I had two tokens
> and a can of tuna at home and an old roll which wouldn't be so bad
> if I warmed it up in the oven and there was some cheese they
>   let me take home
> from the graduate student reading except my roommate had already
>   eaten
> most of it he was pretty good about not touching my stuff but I
>   guess he knew
> this wasn't really "mine" in the sense that I hadn't paid for it
> since it was just rolled up in some party napkins half of it sliced
> the other half a big cube and I had exactly seven dollars in my pocket
> which was my train fare to and from school the next day
> I went to Sarah Lawrence where the flowers were in bloom
> and everyone in the town had shiny blond hair and pastel turtlenecks
> and I tutored a woman who had all her meals catered macrobiotic
> delivered right to her dorm and I knew she'd feel bad for me if she
>   knew
> I ate fish from a can she'd feel bad like my dad did the time
>   he visited me

and he saw my thirty-nine cent chili that I bought from a supermarket
   cart
where they dump all the food with expired codes and the dented cans
and my father said don't eat this you could die of botulism
and I felt like I'd botched up and that botulism was a disease
that hit people like me who didn't have enough to open a checking
   account
who cashed checks and just lived off the money until it was gone. (3)

One can read the "botulism/botched" word play as a confession of shame; the speaker may sense that her flawed character and bad financial planning have caused her life without even "a checking account." Inadvertently reinforced by the father's pity and fear, such shame about the precarious situation of having only "seven dollars in [her] pocket," "two" subway or bus "tokens," inadequate nutrition, and a delayed paycheck clearance entails a barrier to satisfaction, the goal of Spinoza/Altieri's conative force. Frustration and anxiety could either motivate second-order self-assessments that align the speaker with new actions (conative energies) to remove the shame or snowball into hopelessness and reduce the likelihood of positive action. Indeed, selective perception could intensify her dark mood. (E.g., does "everyone in the town" really have "shiny blond hair and pastel turtlenecks," as opposed to the speaker's lackluster locks, due to insufficient funds for regular shampooing and conditioning, and dingy old clothes?)

To invoke Felski's term, readers with an allegiance to the concept of social Darwinism (who think that getting an MFA in creative writing is frivolous) would probably consider the shame justified and would believe that the student should adopt a second-order self-assessment that leads to a new career path. For working-class proponents of social Darwinist ideology, recognition of parallels of their own experience of deprivation would not likely result in empathy for the speaker's emotional suffering. On the other hand, left-leaning readers would want the working-class speaker to display awareness of and challenge large social factors—often addressed in other poems by

Duhamel—influencing economic class situations as much as or more than character traits. In their case, allegiance would facilitate empathy; in some cases, recognition would be present in their identification with the student. (All of these generalizations are subject to exceptions and to other factors.)

In the second strophe's first sentence, framing of what previously seemed the present as happening in the past briefly creates a distancing effect: "it's easy to feel sorry for my former self ..." (4). In *not* pitying her "former self," the present self suggests that it has adopted a more satisfactory attitude, but the speaker goes on to recount more details that *could* encourage pity for "the one that wanted to go to grad school so bad she" took on various low-paying jobs and spent her $200 life savings on a "clunker" "that died" almost at once and, according to a mechanic, would take nearly five times the cost to fix. As the long sentence continues, it appears that the speaker is recollecting the most intense point of the former self's frustration and anxiety:

> ... so she just junked it and refused to eat
> because everything she tried was an ugly mistake a sour bargain
> and there was no way she could get ahead or even make the time to feel
>   her angst
> to write a good workshop poem since she had to be at her job at five
> in the morning where she was a receptionist in a health club
> and they gave her a big gold key that looked like a key to the city ... (3–4)

The funny passage about "Angst" and the "workshop poem" may be hyperbole, but it depicts the former self as so trapped in her scrambling to deal with work, her domestic situation, and school to remain at a subsistence level that the "leisure" to sleep enough hours and process emotions is drastically compromised.

From this nadir, the poem gradually moves toward disputing shame, what Altieri would call a conative adjustment offering a new attitude toward the narrative of how she adjusts to deprivation. There is a potential for reparation. When the "big gold key" that opens the "health club" is said to resemble a "key to the city," it reminds her that not only did she want "to go to grad school so bad[ly]" as access to aesthetic development and a professional career but that living in New York City itself is a part of both. In a cramped, filthy apartment where her roommate holds the lease and, the aspiring poet discovers, pays one-tenth of the rent to her nine-tenths, the speaker "wrote her poems with her typewriter on her lap but still she wrote them and/ she never felt so bad for herself really because she was in New York/ on the corner of First Avenue and First Street where everything began …" (4–5). In a geographical sense, there is a great deal of Manhattan below First and First, but "everything" pertaining to the speaker's dreams "began" for her in that location.

As the sentence quoted above continues, the speaker utters a broad affirmation, "and most of the time she felt like she had everything" (5), without elaboration. Through renewed focus on her long-term goals, she is able to disrupt the negative trajectory of shame. She sharpens conative energies by establishing the kind of person she wants to be: one who chooses challenging goals that require working through a complex array of difficulties and who persists. Thus, all of her numerous calculations and adaptations to money problems and their effect on nutrition, transportation, environment, physical energy, and overall health (including using "coffee and diet pills" [4] to stay awake in a class after severe sleep deprivation) are based on an assessment of a hierarchy of priorities.

The present self represents the former self's awareness of possessing agency, despite so much that is outside her control. This emerges as a source of satisfaction and an indication of the possibility of moving toward greater fulfillment. In pre-laptop days, poems written "with her typewriter on her lap" are "still" poems written. Considering the many images of precarious experience, one can also imagine her realization that her ability to make these choices also involves laboring for a future that, like the $200 car's functionality, is not assured. It takes courage to gamble with basic resources. Further, since her larger decisions involve lengthy (at this point, seemingly endless) postponement of gratifications and constant efforts to ignore scores of inconveniences, she can get away from feeling "so bad for herself" through awareness that she has been developing formidable physical and mental endurance, flexibility in thought and action, and resilience: knowing that there was no "where else/ … to live for $450 a month," she "just" had to "ignore the mother cockroach she saw/ diving in the bread crumbs and the baby cockroaches that scattered/ in the kitchen sink …" (4), among other disgusting sensory experiences. The "cockroach" image is a parody of the image of a fearless, resilient mother skunk that concludes Robert Lowell's "Skunk Hour," a famous "confessional" poem dominated by psychic bleakness.

Like the skunk in Lowell's poem, the image of Duhamel's title "Egg Rolls" enters in the final phase. At the end of the third strophe, "and most of the time she felt like she had everything," is followed by a qualification that runs into the final strophe and leads to the story of a purchase:

> except that time she smelled those egg rolls
> the ones wafting from the Chinese restaurant and she told herself
>
> maybe I should run home and sell my subway tokens to my roommate and walk
> the forty blocks to work tomorrow in the frigid dark and have one of those egg rolls
> the ones with shrimp bits and light green vegetables inside and I fingered
> my seven dollars the five and two ones I carried with me
> just in case the apartment was robbed … (5)

Olfactory pleasure leads to visual pleasure and then a taste thrill for the student poet/health club receptionist whose supervisor had indoctrinated her "about the new diets" (4), which turn out to be ridiculously limited, if economical. When the speaker's simile likens the lines of egg rolls that she sees in the restaurant window to "sleeping bags under fluorescent light," the choice to buy two small egg rolls from "the cook … with a gray ponytail and white bibbed apron" (5) seems to signal a harmless respite from sacrifice, a pleasant, momentary departure from the usual priorities to balance austerity with a bit of enjoyment and accept inconvenience "tomorrow." But as the poem winds down, greater significance is assigned to this action:

> grease burning my lower lip
> the hot insides burning the roof of my mouth you're supposed to drink
>   milk
> that's the only way to cure that scorch something about the protein
> healing the cells of the tongue but I had no milk so I blew into the egg
>   roll
> like a mother blowing on her baby's spoon
> or like a diva testing a microphone and the whole city hushed
> as I squeezed the greasy napkin and it was like I was singing a torch
>   song
> but I wasn't that sad that I wouldn't have the money to go to school
>   tomorrow
> or that my diet was shot and I actually remember feeling kind of rich. (5)

Even the former self's little greasy pleasure involves careful adjustments to pain that she tries to place in grander contexts through a string of similes. As "singing a [celebratory] torch song" and "feeling kind of rich" seem hyperbolic responses to eating some food, this mundane occasion entails celebration of satisfactions that her conative energies make possible. From the perspective of readers who can identify with her through allegiance and/or recognition and/or empathy, she has broken through feelings of shame and hopelessness. The text provides a thorough record of affective and cognitive adaptability to constantly shifting, complex circumstances influenced by class position. She is in the process of becoming a flexible, resourceful person open to diverse experiences. Never succumbing to "sour bargains" or shying away from useful risks, the speaker, in Altieri's terms, has persisted in considering, testing, and at times modifying identifications rather than bowing to externally driven definitions. She often foregoes and at times enjoys small comforts in efforts to gain the larger satisfactions of academic absorption and advancement, engagement in the life of New

York City, and, later, a career as a poet (and professor) that the actual Duhamel has experienced. Readers who do not achieve any of these forms of identification with the poem's speaker could dismiss the poem as self-indulgent or criticize it from an ideological, philosophical, or psychological perspective.

Altieri's theoretical framework and Sedgwick's discussion of reparative reading show that there are potential benefits to emotional identification with a poem and its persona or character beyond the "purging" of passions. Readers can move from absorption in vivid feelings as a primary motivation and initial benefit of the encounter with the text, as Stephanie Burt sketches, to what Edwin Creeley calls "interpretive framing of self" that results in those readers' own conative adjustments. And it is also possible that in a poem, a character's conative adjustment can go wrong and move in a destructive direction rather than in a healthful one—for example, in Robert Browning's "My Last Duchess," where the duke's narcissism turns him into a killer. In such cases, readers can progress from identification to a thoughtful *withdrawal from* identification and can understand what kind of pattern to avoid.

In some cases, readers who might otherwise be put off by a poem's linguistic complexity or would perceive the manner of presentation as "pretentious" detect and then identify strongly with the complicated emotion(s) represented and are motivated to work through difficulties and develop an appreciation for its artistry. Stephanie Burt cogently describes this phenomenon in discussing the appeal of John Donne's metaphysical love poem, "A Valediction Forbidding Mourning": "If you yourself have ever felt unique, or confused, or confusing to others, especially in matters of the heart" or believed that a "connection to somebody else … deserves a passionate defense … you might see Donne's elaborate, challenging metaphors not as barriers to sincerity but as ways to achieve it" (19).

There are students who are driven by fascination with otherness and its mysteries. They prove eager to encounter and ponder emotional situations that do *not* elicit their political or ethical allegiance, recognition, or even, at first, their empathy. Psychology, sociology, and human services majors especially come to mind. As Stephanie Burt puts it, "sometimes the pleasure in reading lyric poems involves discovering structures of feeling you have never encountered, or never understood" (34–35). A reader from an economically privileged background who can have an egg roll (or caviar) at any time without negative consequences might be jolted into curiosity about the speaker's affective experiences in Duhamel's "Egg Rolls," and a monolingual English speaker who encounters Paolo Javier's "Feeling Its Actual" might suddenly consider the challenges of American English for an immigrant thrust into an alien linguistic and cultural environment.

Curiosity about an author's autobiographical or biographical context can motivate students to work harder at trying to comprehend a challenging poem. A few months before teaching an English version of Brazilian poet Adélia Prado's "Successive Deaths," I had a chance meeting on a bus with Prado's translator, Ellen Doré Watson. In the course of the conversation, I learned from Watson that the three deaths of family members (sister, mother, and father—the first two coming early in her life) that are narrated in the poem actually befell Prado. When I relayed this to my students, many of them took the poem very seriously, perhaps because they trusted a record of actual events of extremity, however poeticized, more than they would just another fiction, as Prado's emotional truth.

Prado places great emphasis on the emotional component of her poetry. In a visit with her, Watson recalls asking the poet about the most important point to consider while translating her work into English: "Be faithful to the emotion that generated the original, she said. Don't be clever; let yourself get carried away; re-create feelings, not words" (xiv). "Successive Deaths" has a clear narrative trajectory, moving from quick recovery from the first grief, to slower recovery from the second, to the assertion that healing from the third has not occurred, as well as a tone of unmistakably deepening sadness; nevertheless, it is not a transparent record of emotions. I would suggest that ambiguous language, reiteration of tropes/images, and a concluding allusion complicate Prado's "re-creation" of "feelings" for readers.

The poem begins: "When my sister died, I cried a great deal/ and was quickly consoled. There was a new dress/ and a thicket in the back yard where I could exist" (4). Few readers would have trouble perceiving the "new dress" as a consolation for the young child or playing in the thicket as a distraction, but the verb "exist" when set in relation to "thicket" may give pause. The sister does not exist in the world; the speaker continues to do so. However, if no one in a given class has a decent knowledge of Brazilian Portuguese, then they will not be able to say whether "to exist" is compared unfavorably with or merely equivalent to "to live." Also, readers can only make conjectures about the emotional connotation(s) of "thicket" for Prado, if they are seeking active intention. A thicket can provide enclosure, a form of protection, like a hiding place, or it can resemble a grave, and the idea that it may have brambles that can sting someone could also be relevant to an understanding of the speaker's affect at this stage of the narrative.

The poem's second death, the mother's, coincides with the speaker's awkward physical rite of passage:

> When my mother died, I was consoled more slowly.
> There was a newfound uneasiness:
> my breasts were shaped like two hillocks
> and I was quite naked.
> I crossed my arms over them when I cried. (4)

The girl whose breasts are just starting to grow can be distracted from grief by her "newfound uneasiness." Readers might conclude that the adjective "naked" is not quite literal—that using "arms" as "clothing" for a part of the body is not the same as having actual clothing hide most of the body.

The treatment of the third death, the father's, occupies well over half of the poem, and it gets tougher to interpret near the end. First, the speaker declares: "When my father died, I was never again consoled" (4). This powerful declaration is followed by a list of the speaker's efforts to bolster her memory of her father through "old pictures, ... acquaintances,/ relatives who would remind" her of his specific characteristics. She even "imitated the way his body curled/ in his last sleep and repeated the words/ he said when I touched his feet:/ 'Never mind, they're all right.'" The class can discuss the poignancy of the use of metonymy to attempt to recover the father's "presence."

Next, "Who will console me?" seems a rhetorical question that harks back to the clause, "I was never again consoled." The poem's last three lines include the repetition of two key tropes/images, as well as the verb "exist," and another trope conveying an allusion to the Old Testament: "My breasts fulfilled their promise/ and the thicket where I exist/ is the genuine burning bush of memory." When readers think about how the "breasts" are an important trope for different stages in life that reflect the movement from slow consolation to being inconsolable, they face another ambiguity. Does the notion of "promise" merely indicate that the woman's breasts are fully developed and therefore she is mature enough not to be distracted from the reality of her loss? Or does it suggest that, by the time of her father's death, she has given milk to her own children and, therefore, understands the true preciousness of parents, especially mothers, better than she did when the "hillocks" were just emerging?

As the earlier physical thicket is displaced by a mental one, the drift of the poem suggests that to "exist" in an environment without consolation seems tougher than to "exist" in one with even trivial solace: the speaker must now dwell in her memory rather than in the actual present. However, the reader has no external evidence to decide whether the adjective "genuine" in the concluding line signals some sort of positive spiritual result, a degree of reparation if not full consolation for the three losses, or whether "genuine" merely means "actual" or "true." And a reader could tie Prado's use of the "burning bush" to details of the narrative in Exodus in more than one way. The bush, which continually burns without being turned into ashes, is represented in the Old Testament as a sacred scene of divine instruction, where the deity orders Moses to assume the task of leading his people out of Egypt. When he demurs because of his lack of oratorical prowess, Aaron is provided as a spokesperson. Does the use of the allusion tell us that the place of memory is sacred and the imperative to pursue memory is "divine," intensely painful but not ultimately destructive to the ongoing mourner, whose mourning "burns" her but also purifies (purges) and redeems her? Is the muse of poetry the "spokesperson" for the poet, who would otherwise be unable to put into words the enormity of her grief and the most essential aspects of memory? Is the divine command to lead the exodus from Egypt a symbol for the speaker leading herself to memory as a "genuine" experience of the presence of those who are physically absent and, thus, the consolation that she previously said is impossible? Or does the speaker's "existence" "in" "the burning bush" constitute ongoing agony without reparation? Readers immersed in what they perceive as Prado's autobiographical poetic narrative can find a great deal of emotional resonance in "Successive Deaths" whether or not they feel able to support answers to these and other questions.

It is a truism of pedagogy that a reader should be skeptical about the correspondence between the "I" in a poem and the poet. I tend to repeat it in every class whenever tenuous assumptions arise. Yet the admonition need not come immediately. If a student's tentative imagining of this connection motivates interest in the poem prior to writing about it, I don't want to squelch that motivation but prefer to explore each possibility. Sometimes, strong external evidence shows that the correspondence does not hold, but it is useful to point out that poets who don't exhibit the programmatic or active intention to do "life writing" may compose texts "collaging" elements of their own direct experience, along with others' experience and fiction gained from various media.

As for situations where a speaker/poet connection enjoys widespread agreement among professional scholars, an instructor should inform students about clashes over *how* autobiographical elements shape overall understanding of poems. After all, one should carefully examine differing conjectures about the autobiographical features of a poem. When I consider conflicts about the impact of allusion in W.B. Yeats's "A Prayer for My Daughter" in my third chapter, I will also show that these differences in critical perspective hinge substantially on biographical data. Further, a good safeguard against settling on facile, broad generalizations about (auto)biographically tinged meaning is to invoke the possibility, raised in Chapter 1, of unconscious interference with active and final intentions. Referring to his celebrated 1959 "confessional" volume *Life Studies*, Robert Lowell speaks of "a good deal of tinkering with fact. You leave out a lot, and emphasize this and not that. Your actual experience is a complete flux" (21). He admits to having "invented facts and changed things," but adds: "if a poem is autobiographical …, you want the reader to say, this is true … [T] here was always that standard of truth which you wouldn't ordinarily have in poetry—the reader was to believe he was getting the *real* Robert Lowell."

Fueled by identification with the author, students write effective essays that use (auto)biographical evidence to support their reading of a poem. I also find it useful to guide them to perceive, if applicable, a poet's likely motives for a particular style of self-presentation that may exclude other plausible kinds. Writers also sometimes include in their poems a recognition that thorough objectivity about their experience and its impact on identity seems impossible.

History, political science, sociology, and anthropology majors who are deeply committed to their discipline tend to be eager to gain knowledge about cultural perspectives other than their own; accompanying this intellectual component is frequently an affective one. They may view speakers and characters as exemplars of cultural formations and want to identify how social practices and historical circumstances elicit particular emotional responses. For example, a sociology student might want to research attitudes toward death in Brazilian Catholic culture (as I have not done) before drawing any conclusions from a close reading of Prado's "Successive Deaths." I have found that some of these students regard the relative brevity of poetic analysis, including the tracking of allusions, useful for this purpose. Immersion in their discipline could cause some of them to discuss and write about the poem in a way that ignores poetic attributes aside from culturally charged allusions, or they might not pay attention to details that seem to go against their sociopolitical stance. In fact, if a writer gets carried away with external historical, political, or sociological evidence, s/he might make internal evidence a small portion of the essay's argument. I attempt to set clear, precise guidelines for the first draft of an essay so that these kinds of things do not happen. And if the guidelines do not sink in, specific comments on the first graded draft about areas in which the student needs to demonstrate *how* the poem communicates (rather than just *what* it communicates) can help the writer compose an effective revision. These comments can be reinforced in a conference.

I believe in taking students' emotional aversion to a poem's speaker or to their impression of a poet as seriously as its opposite, identification/attachment. Aversion can stem from a reader's sense that s/he is being manipulated by the poet's use of heavy-handed rhetoric or misleading narrative inclusions and omissions. A reader can also stand in opposition to the author's perceived cultural or political ideology (the reverse of Rita Felski's "allegiance," cited earlier), or find the speaker's "personality" disagreeable, often influenced by the memory of actual encounters. In general, negative moral judgment can cause antipathy for the poem and poet. Although Felski refers to "ironic identification" stemming from "shared dissociation" as a cause of attachment, the poet's attempt to enlist the reader's approbation of a sense of dissociation's moral superiority can backfire and engender resentment when the latter has positive associations about the situation that the former ironizes.

At times, I've found that a student with an intensely felt aversion resisted any effort on my part to engage openly with a particular poem. However, I sometimes encourage the student to channel and refine this negative passion into the development of a precise aesthetic and/or ethical, political, or psychological critique grounded in close attention to most of the poem's details. This approach works when students grasp an opportunity to be true to their feelings *and* simultaneously immerse themselves in elaborate, precise, coherent interpretation.

It is also valuable to help students learn to cultivate a double perspective: to critique what one feels is flawed about a poem and to look for, analyze, and evaluate more generative, affirmable elements. Much of the time, this isn't equivocation or indecisiveness; it bespeaks a critical maturity that acknowledges the actual complexity of multiple contexts and criteria. In defense of "close reading" and its emphasis on "small details" as a "safeguard against projection" and "preconceptions" about a text's "main idea or general shape" (11), Jane Gallop counsels resistance against both the assumption that the text "is great, wise, admirable, and [to] read it lovingly, looking for instances of its wisdom, ignoring those things that seem wrong or off to us" and the assumption that it "is bad, stupid, dangerous, and [to] read it aggressively looking for examples of its stupidity, ignoring those things that we might actually like or agree with" ("The Ethics of Reading: Close Encounters," 16). Gallop indicates that temporary suspension of judgment until after a careful reading of a text will "help the student learn better" and "make her sharper and more adaptable, prepare her better for the surprises thrown in her path" (12). On the other hand, "fighting prejudice with prejudice" (16) is a dead end. Noting that "literary studies" appropriately "embraced historicism as part of a rejection of timeless universals," Gallop wants historicists to realize that "close reading poses an ongoing threat to easy, reductive generalization," to "smug, overarching conclusions" ("The Historicization of Literary Studies," 185).

If a professor sounds preachy in conveying Gallop's advice, students will often respond with irony, outright sarcasm, or lifeless lip service. In class discussion and office-hour conferences, specific questions implicitly introducing alternative views or attitudes are the most effective way to reach students who passionately adhere to aesthetic, ethical, or ideological concepts resulting in aversion to a speaker or author. Such questions would also enhance the quality of engagement of those who are so attached to the narrative, characterization, or abstract concepts of the poem that, in Gallop's terms, they miss many of the "small details" and have a rosy, cloudy impression of the "main idea or general shape."

3

Crossroads of Interpretation

Stanley Fish declares: "The discovery of the 'real point' is always what is claimed whenever a new interpretation is advanced, but the claim makes sense only in relation to a point (or points) that had previously been considered the real one" (350). "The conventions of the institution," Fish continues, dictate that "the space in which a critic works has been marked out for him [*sic*] by his predecessors," since there is an "unwritten requirement that an interpretation present itself as remedying a deficiency" in prior readings. On the one hand, the march of interpretations of a poem over the years in academic criticism may seem to be a progression toward greater and greater understanding based on synchronous and asynchronous collaboration of scholars united in a desire for truth. On the other hand, as I suggested in my discussion of intention in the first chapter, we do not have access to a set of immutable laws of reading against which some "supreme court" can measure "progress" objectively. At any given time, interpreters with differing aesthetic and ideological interests and theoretical orientations make their divergent cases and continue to disagree.

In group work and class discussion that take place in a literature course, I find that, aside from eliciting students' interpretive conjectures, it is often beneficial to expose them to various components of others' interpretations and rationales for them—including implicit and explicit interpretive frames. (If no one has published criticism on the poem, I devise alternative readings.) This staged clash of two or more interpretations gives students raw material to arrive at their own views after careful inspection of the poem's language, reflection on the impact of formal elements, and attention to external evidence accompanied by thorough consideration of rival claims. In each of the six examples that follow, I neither present my own reading nor supply a transcript of a class discussion about the poem in question but sketch ways in which interpretations differ from one another.

In "A Prayer for My Daughter," William Butler Yeats's speaker lyrically expresses the heartfelt prayer that the baby crying in her cradle grows up to follow a particular set of precepts. It is difficult to dissociate the speaker from Yeats himself, as he wrote the poem the year his daughter, Anne Butler Yeats, was born (1919). So it would seem odd to exclude biographical and historical evidence and a search for conscious intention, even if unconscious forces might be important.

Yeats was writing shortly after the First World War armistice, during the Spanish Flu pandemic, and during the armed struggle with Great Britain that finally resulted in the compromise establishment of the Irish Free State as a member of the British Commonwealth in 1921. Thus, it makes sense that the first two octaves speak of "the great gloom that is on [his] mind" (20) and are full of spooky portents. In addition, when the speaker's "excited reverie" fastens upon the arrival of "the future years," "dancing to a frenzied drum,/ Out of the murderous innocence of the sea," it reflects Yeats's understanding that the world was heading toward apocalypse in the year 2000, as indicated in "The Second Coming," the poem right before "A Prayer for My Daughter" in *Michael Robartes and the Dancer* (1921). He fully developed this understanding in *A Vision* (1925). (The actual Anne Butler Yeats died on US Independence Day in 2001.)

In 1983, the novelist Joyce Carol Oates voices what is now a common perspective on Yeats's poem: a feminist critique of the poet's conscious intention to inflict patriarchal ideas on his female child. Oates identifies "Yeats's first concern for his daughter [as] her physical appearance" (16), as evidenced by the third stanza:

May she be granted beauty and yet not
Beauty to make a stranger's eye distraught,
Or hers before a looking-glass, for such,
Being made beautiful overmuch,

Consider beauty a sufficient end,
Lose natural kindness and maybe
The heart-revealing intimacy
That chooses right, and never find a friend. (21)

Oates associates Yeats's opposition to this disquietingly intense beauty with fear that it "might arouse in her a sense of her own autonomy: her existence in a 'looking-glass' rather than in a man's eyes" (16). Examples in the next stanza confirm the idea that Yeats holds (not merely entertains) a stereotype that those women who are "made beautiful overmuch" tend to lack "natural kindness":

Helen being chosen found life flat and dull
And later had much trouble from a fool,
While that great Queen, that rose out of the spray,
Being fatherless could have her way
Yet chose a bandy-leggèd smith for man.
It's certain that fine women eat
A crazy salad with their meat
Whereby the Horn of Plenty is undone. (21)

Oates maintains that the poem is Yeats's "instrument of revenge" (18) against Maud Gonne, the British-born revolutionary on behalf of the Irish cause. Yeats could never win her love. He identifies her with Helen of Troy in various poems, such as "No Second Troy." According to Marjorie Perloff, the phrase "much trouble from a fool" refers to Gonne's brief, difficult marriage to fellow revolutionary John MacBride, for whom Yeats had contempt—until MacBride's martyrdom in the Easter Uprising that caused a partial reappraisal in "Easter, 1916" ('"The Tradition of Myself,'" 552). Indeed, Anne's very existence was a result of the poet's 1917 rebound marriage to Georgie Hyde-Lees after Gonne rejected Yeats for the last time and then her daughter Iseult also turned down his proposal. Although "no direct references to Maud Gonne" appear in the poem, Perloff calls her its "dominant figure." She asserts that "contrasts" presented in "A Prayer"—what Oates calls "the crude division between good girl and shrill [hysterical?] woman" (19)—"are so carefully developed that the speaker's choice between two kinds of women appears as a universal human choice, not just the poem's own" (Perloff, "'The Tradition of Myself,'" 553). Yet Perloff reads this patriarchal positing of "universality" as a front for the personal score the poet wants to settle. Finding "desperation in Yeats's willed insistence on the expiation of hatred" ("Between Hatred and Desire," 42), Perloff perceives in the poem, written soon after a serious altercation with Gonne, a "willed regression ... in which Yeats tries to convince Maud Gonne that he no longer wants or adores her" (44).

From Perloff's perspective, Yeats uses "A Prayer" as a reparative act that serves, whether he intended it to or not, to fortify patriarchal ideology in general. In *The Resisting Reader: A Feminist Approach to American Fiction* (1978), Judith Fetterly foregrounds the power of emotional identification and identifies how "the female reader is coopted into participation in an experience from which she is explicitly excluded" and is "seduced" into self-defeating identification "with a selfhood that defines itself in opposition to her" (xii). The literature that she analyzes manipulates sympathy for men and a negative view toward women involved with them. The critic regards "this refusal to assent" to such manipulation as the beginning of "the process of exorcizing the male mind that has been implanted in us" (xxii). Now, more than four decades after the publication of Fetterly's book, it is much easier for readers in general to resist emotional identification with or empathy for the poet-speaker's effort at reparation if they read it as Oates and Perloff do. But soon, we will find that one critic believes that reparation for Yeats does not depend on masculinist coercion.

The poet/speaker in the fifth stanza of "A Prayer for My Daughter" continues to focus on virtues of a woman possessing a moderate degree of beauty, including the implications for marriage prospects: "In courtesy I'd have her chiefly learned;/ hearts are not had as a gift but hearts are earned/ By those what are not entirely beautiful ..." (22). Elizabeth Butler Cullingford, who pursues a feminist critique while also noting elements in the poem that do not neatly fit patriarchal ideology, considers it "refreshing" that Yeats posits "the 'not entirely beautiful' woman as an ideal," as he replaces "courtly frustration" with "kindness and friendship as the model of male/female relations" (136). Cullingford also appreciates "the notion of love as a gradual development rather than a thunderbolt"; she refers to the evocation of "a mature and sympathetic relationship" through the implied "depiction of George Yeats" and her significance to the poet. In her analysis Oates does not refer to Anne's mother at all. Cullingford's point is plausible, since Yeats is one who has "played the fool/ For beauty's very self" (Gonne), having "roved,/ Loved and thought himself beloved," and is finally "made wise" in being unable to "take his eyes" from Georgie's "glad kindness" (Yeats 186).

Oates's gloss on the sixth octave, in which Yeats adds other prescriptions about curbing of self-expression and travel to the ones about "courtesy" and "kindness," is that "the female is not to concern herself with history, with action; it is her role simply to exist" (18). Here is the octave:

> May she become a flourishing hidden tree
> That all her thoughts may like the linnet be,
> And have no business but dispensing round
> Their magnaminities of sound,
> Nor but in merriment begin a chase,
> Nor but in merriment a quarrel.
> O may she live like some green laurel
> Rooted in one dear perpetual place. (22)

Oates maintains that Yeats "would have his daughter an object in nature for others'—which is to say male—delectation," and she "is to be brainless and voiceless, *rooted*" (17). Alternatively, Cullingford asserts that Yeats's desire for Anne's security is "understandable in the immediate historical context of war and political instability" but "[purchases] safety at the price of sequestration" (136). Further, calling attention to the image (which will return at the poem's end) of a laurel tree, she regards it as an "allusion to the rape narrative of Apollo and Daphne," in which Daphne's father Peneus transforms her into a laurel to fulfill her request to "remain a virgin forever rather than" submit to Apollo's lust, thereby "preserving her chastity at the expense of her humanity" (137). Cullingford then links it with another allusion: "The idea of a single life is reinforced by the allusion to Wordsworth's 'The Green Linnet,' a bird that is 'Too blest with any one to pair;/ Thyself thy own enjoyment.'" Brenda Maddox, who briefly discusses the poem in a biography about Yeats while entertaining a feminist viewpoint, accepts Cullingford's assumption that the "laurel" image refers to Peneus's metamorphic gesture. However, she interprets the significance of the allusion differently—as evidence of "incestuous thoughts that a daughter can stir in a father (and that Iseult Gonne roused in Yeats and her stepfather, John MacBride)" and, more generally, of the idea that "the arrival of a daughter suddenly raised the specter of [Yeats's] guilty lust for young women" (144).

Ruth Vanita, herself a feminist critic and queer theorist, considers "A Prayer for My Daughter" "a reverie on the nature of the self," especially "in the sense of the universal spirit, as Yeats used the term in his translation of ... the *Upanishads.*" Vanita begins the gist of her argument against Oates and Cullingford's views of the poem through a careful reading of the sixth stanza. Like the feminist critics, she invokes external evidence, both intertextual and biographical, but the allusions are entirely different ones. She contends that "Yeats invokes cross-cultural tropes, ... to bring the Upanishadic understanding of the self into relation with everyday life" (239). Vanita cites poems by Robert Burns, Alfred Lord Tennyson, Robert Bridges, and another poem by Wordsworth, "The Tables Turned," as well as a short story by Oscar Wilde (241–243), to point out that "the female linnet in English poetry generally appears as a mother while the male linnet is free and self-delighting" (241). She considers Wordsworth's linnet to be "male" (242) and suggests that Yeats may be "the first major English [*sic*] poet" to have "feminiz[ed] this symbol of freedom and joyful creativity" and spirituality (243).

Further, Vanita posits a different allusive context from Cullingford's reading of the laurel. For her, the tree symbolizes, "as in Yeats's translation of the *Isha Upanishad*, universal Self or spirit" (243), not merely an individual ego. She cites "Yeats's and Purohit Swami's translation of the *Prashna Upanishad*: 'All things fly to the Self, as birds fly to the tree for rest,'" as well as the *Chhandogya Upanishad*: "'A tethered bird, after flying in every direction, settles down on its perch; the mind, after wandering in every direction, settles down on its life; for … mind is tethered to life.'" And she states that the bird in Yeats's poem "spontaneously flies to the tree that constitutes its life." As for Greco-Roman mythological significations, Vanita finds the laurel's "association with Apollo" as a "symbol of creativity and knowledge, hence the crowning of poets with laurel wreaths" in line with "the poem's exploration of spiritual damage and recovery" (247). Cullingford and Maddox would probably counter that the god's attempted rape of Daphne is more central to this context than positive associations with Apollo. Vanita refers to the laurel as a self-regenerating evergreen and notes that "in the Bible and in Roman culture," it symbolizes "prosperity, victory and fame, hence the laurel wreath worn by victors" and the later "symbol of Christ's resurrection." Also, for this critic, "Daphne's laurel" does not signify "chastity" but "autonomy." Since Yeats refers to "some green laurel," Vanita associates "green, the color of modern Irish nationalism … with the heroine's freedom and joy." Noting that Anne in the future is figured as "both laurel and linnet" and deeming her "both rooted and free," she believes that the double trope signifies "the oneness of the individual self (the bird) with the universal Self (the 'holy tree' growing in the heart of all beings)" (248).

In glossing the poem's seventh and eighth stanzas, Oates/Cullingford and Vanita clash over the significance of "hate"/"hatred" and being "opinionated." Yeats's speaker in the seventh octave declares "that to be choked with hate/ May well be of all evil chances chief" and concludes that "If there's no hatred in a mind/ Assault and battery of the wind/ Can never tear the linnet from the leaf" (23). In the eighth stanza, the speaker underscores the deleterious effects of hatred *for women*:

An intellectual hatred is the worst,
So let her think opinions are accursed.
Have I not seen the loveliest woman born
Out of the mouth of Plenty's horn,

Because of her opinionated mind
Barter that horn and every good
By quiet natures understood
For an old bellows full of angry wind? (22)

Cullingford finds the denunciation of "the 'screaming' woman of ideas ... shrill in tone and unjust to Gonne's public activities; it marks a regression in Yeats's acceptance of changing gender roles" (136). The source of Yeats's attitude, Cullingford observes, is a deep sociopolitical anxiety: "Irish events in the aftermath of the [Easter] rising confirmed the association between women and extreme politics," especially "the widows and bereft mothers of the revolution," and so, thanks to pressure, "in February 1918 the franchise was granted to women over thirty, and women stood for parliament for the first time" (135). Yeats's old friend and a subject in other poems, the activist Constance Markievicz, though "still in jail ... united Republican, suffragist, and labor support to win a seat in the House of Commons." Maud Gonne, a major figure in the radical movement for Irish independence who endured exile and prison terms for her beliefs, sometimes clashed with Yeats over their political positions. Therefore, Yeats's aim in the poem, Cullingford states, is "to protect his daughter from the violence that these beautiful women seemed to foment or attract" (135).

We should also consider the context of Yeats's engagement with Irish nationalism by utilizing postcolonial criticism's attention to colonial subjects' degrees of accommodation and resistance to their situation. Referring to Yeats's early involvement in the independence-seeking Irish Republican Brotherhood, perhaps largely due to his desire to win Maud Gonne, Stephen Regan debunks the idea that Yeats was an anticolonial "hero"; the poet "came from a Protestant family with strong ties to the so-called Anglo-Irish 'ascendancy' or governing class, at a time when 'revolutionary' nationalism was being promoted most vociferously by Catholic intellectuals such as Patrick Pearse" (89). Regan argues that "the nationalism that Yeats espouses in the 1890s, far from being 'revolutionary,' ... emerges from a deep sense of cultural insecurity and … anxiety about his own embattled social class" (96). Yeats's "complex Protestant consciousness," he claims, made him "reject the worst excesses of English administration in Ireland and at the same time remain committed to the British Empire" (98). Regan doubts that the poet "ever seriously entertained the idea of complete separation from England"—beyond "Home Rule" involving membership in the Commonwealth. Instead, Yeats sought to develop "powerful and enduring myths of Irishness that might shape a new national consciousness" producing "a distinctive cultural and spiritual identity, an imagined community free of sectarian differences and conflicts." This "vision" was no longer "democratic," since the poet "became more contemptuous towards Catholic aspirations in the first decade of the twentieth century." If Regan's adjective "contemptuous" is accurate, then contempt might mask fear of an eventual erosion of the rights of Protestants in Ireland. (Ireland did not leave the commonwealth and establish itself as an independent republic until 1949, ten years after Yeats's death.)

A postcolonial or Marxist critic who considers an account of material conditions as the most significant external evidence would consider the articulation of patriarchal ideology of secondary importance in active intentions animating the poet/speaker's verse argument. What Yeats in 1919 may find most unpalatable about Maud Gonne, who was, in fact, "born/ Out of the mouth of Plenty's horn," and other Catholic revolutionary women in Ireland is that their "intellectual hatred" and political "opinions" would endanger socioeconomic stability and an acceptable level of Irish self-government. He probably fears greater oppression by Great Britain, as well as greater polarization between the Catholic majority and Protestant minority. Yeats may see his own political perspective as "reason" and the radical women's solely as the product of violent emotion ("angry wind") to be discounted as mere "opinion." Thus, he may ignore his own emotional investments and the possible utility of some of the radicals' strategies, including deployment and eliciting of intense emotion, to achieve common goals. (Ironically, though, in a recent article, "Reconsidering Maud Gonne," Marjorie

Perloff finds that new scholarship has unearthed the idea that Yeats's towering inamorata was influenced by fascist ideas early in life that never quite loosened their grip. For example, unlike Yeats, she exhibited anti-Jewish prejudices.)

Vanita doesn't go into detail about the Irish historical context that I've just discussed. Examining the eighth octave, she rejects the "conflation of ideas with opinions" (248). Underscoring Oscar Wilde's influence on Yeats, she cites Wilde's "distinction between the play of ideas and the violence of opinion" and asserts that the latter's threat to the former "is not ... specific to women" and that Gonne merely provides the poet with an example. Vanita points to the "ungendered" phrase "quiet natures" to indicate Yeats's belief that everyone should participate in rational discussion, not loud polemic. But should this particular lack of gender reference (and a few in other stanzas) be accorded greater significance than the various references to women in this stanza and most others? Or can one conclude that the poem is not consistent in this regard?

The penultimate stanza describes the benefits of not embracing "an old bellows full of angry wind":

> Considering this, all hatred driven hence,
> The soul recovers radical innocence
> And learns at last that it is self-delighting,
> Self-appeasing, self-affrighting,
> And that its own sweet will is Heaven's will;
> She can, though every face should scowl
> And every windy quarter howl
> Or every bellows burst, be happy still. (23)

Once more, Oates and Cullingford part company. While Oates considers the third and fourth lines above to indicate that "the feminine soul must ... [affect] a kind of autism of the spirit" (18), Cullingford reads this stanza as "briefly constitut[ing] the woman as a subject" who can achieve "spiritual independence" (137) before the speaker takes this "gift" away in the final octave. Oates does not choose to distinguish between mastering one's emotions in order to exercise reason and being stripped of feeling altogether. Against Cullingford's view that this stanza is a temporary endorsement of female spiritual empowerment, Vanita perceives it as "a logical culmination of the poem's argument," "a self-contained sentence with a meaning that does not depend on what went before" (249). She maintains that the pronoun "she" in the sixth line, which had previously referred to Anne, "now also refers to the soul—any soul." However, the noun "soul" in the second line is the antecedent of the pronoun "it" in the third and the possessive pronoun "its" in the fifth line, so it is more likely that "she" still refers to the subject of Yeats's prayer, but perhaps as an exemplar of any soul.

In her reparative reading, Vanita stresses "the word 'recovers'" to point to the soul's loss and regaining of "innocence," just as "the laurel … dies down to its roots and grows again" (249). "Radical," attached here to "innocence," signifies roots/rootedness in Latin, and Vanita adds that in "Latin *nocere*" means "to injure," so "'innocence' … means not harmful, not injurious." For her, the poem's "climax" focuses "on the soul recovering its innate non-harmful nature" (250). Vanita cites passages from the *Chhandogya* and *Brihadaranyaka Upanishads* to support the notion that the trope of "a wounded tree" is used to signify spiritual regeneration, and she stresses that the first three lines of the seventh stanza ("My mind … / … has dried up of late") manifest not only the speaker's prayer for his daughter but his sense of his own predicament and the need for reparation. Countering Oates's interpretation of spiritual autism in the succession of three gerunds preceded by "self," she perceives the passages as an echo of the *Isha Upanishad*'s idea of "self-dependence" and in the *Gita*'s concept of the individual self fundamentally connected with all other selves being able to achieve satisfaction "within the Self alone" (251). Regarding "self-dependence" as a spiritual property, Vanita might have further strengthened her argument if, in opposition to Oates's reading of the third stanza, noted earlier, she observed that Yeats negates the concept of physical "beauty" as "a sufficient end" to steer Anne away from narcissistic tendencies that would contribute to unsatisfactory relationships with other people in general.

"A Prayer for My Daughter" concludes with the affirmation of "custom" and "ceremony," including marriage, as the means of reparation and transcendence of "arrogance and hatred":

> And may her bridegroom bring her to a house
> Where all's accustomed, ceremonious;
> For arrogance and hatred are the wares
> Peddled in the thoroughfares.
> How but in custom and in ceremony
> Are innocence and beauty born?
> Ceremony's a name for the rich horn,
> And custom for the spreading laurel tree. (Yeats 23)

"So crushingly conventional is Yeats's imagination," writes Oates, that he must "conclude his prayer" (17) with the anticipation of Anne's far-distant marriage. Maddox succinctly characterizes Yeats's desire for Anne to have "all the constraints of nineteenth century womanhood … above all … a husband with a Big House and a private income …" (143). Cullingford reads the rhetorical question in the fifth and sixth lines as a pun involving "born"/"borne" (endurance through the role of motherhood despite tough circumstances) that signifies "the idea of woman as the reproducer"—literally and figuratively—"of the ideals and values of a patriarchal society" (138). I have already quoted Cullingford and Maddox's points about sinister implications of the laurel tree. The fact that "the laurel tree [is] the last image of the poem" suggests "the incestuous structure of patriarchal marriage" because, "although formally [the speaker] releases his daughter to the bridegroom, he invites her to return to him and to the imprisonment of the laurel tree" (Cullingford 138–139). Again, Cullingford's interpretation of the laurel as an allusion to the Peneus/Daphne/Apollo myth provides the basis to turn what could otherwise be seen as a structural metaphor with connotations of positive natural growth into a trope of patriarchal captivity.

Vanita claims that "the weight of the preceding stanza" gives the final one a sense of "completion through self-integration" (254) rather than capitulation to patriarchal values. She bases her claim on the *Upanishads*, in which "bride and groom, nature and spirit, are … two dimensions of the same Self, as imaged in the icon of Shiva." She believes that "ceremony" in the poem's final octave conveys "ritual" like "the Vedic *yajna*" to promote the cultivation of "abundance and prosperity" (Vanita 252). Vanita's statement that "tradition and custom arise from rootedness in the universal Self and in a community" (252–253) clinches her reparative reading. Nevertheless, a feminist reader can counter that, if Yeats is actually alluding to Hindu symbolism, he is appropriating it to bolster the authority of his patriarchal imperatives.

"A Prayer for My Daughter" is a text saturated with possible allusions. We have seen readers disagree about what specific allusions are really "present" "in" a word or phrase or clause and which are arbitrarily posited. Here, the range of possible allusions to classical and more recent mystical Western texts, subcontinental spiritual texts, and the historical contexts of the struggle for Irish independence and their intersection with Yeats's life is extremely broad. Imagine if a practitioner of data-mining "distant reading," which Franco Moretti has done much to popularize, performed a digital analysis that found a great many more literary references to "laurel" and even "linnet" in world literature than Cullingford and Vanita did. How would one decide "objectively" which allusions are relevant?

Yeats did not provide substantial external evidence by recording in prose an explanation for particular allusions or his rationale for deploying them. Identification of any of his allusions among numerous possible choices and of their significance in the poem is a matter of conjecture. I would surmise that Cullingford based her linkage of his "laurel" trope to the Peneus/Daphne/Apollo myth on the likelihood that he would be well aware of the myth and that this association with "laurel" fits her impression of his rhetorical purpose. In the case of Vanita's assertions about allusions to the *Upanishads*, Yeats's status as a translator makes many of her ideas plausible, although "tree" (as opposed to "laurel") is an extremely overdetermined trope.

Part of Vanita's impetus in writing her essay is to counter critics who are pejorative about Yeats's involvement with Hinduism by demonstrating that "Yeats's engagement with Indian philosophy" (255) deserves thoughtful consideration. This may be why she offers no specifics about the poet's relationship with Maud and Iseult Gonne or Irish politics as external evidence, since others have covered these areas. Yet critics like Cullingford who perform a feminist reading of "A Prayer for My Daughter" would insist that such evidence is crucial for an understanding of the poem's promotion of patriarchal ideology. In turn, Vanita's argument against the feminist critique rests substantially on other critics' omission of any reference to the influence of the *Upanishads* on Yeats's thinking and use of tropes, as well as her different interpretation of allusions stemming from European culture.

Is it possible for a reader to conclude that the analyses of Oates, Cullingford, Perloff, and Vanita hold true for particular *parts* of "A Prayer for My Daughter"? If so, the poem can be said to disclose Yeats's contradictory impulses about freedom and constraint, physical "rootedness" and intellectual/spiritual mobility, generosity and self-protection, individual needs and collective needs, universal and historical particularities. From this perspective, the poem is a busy "thoroughfare" that reflects the daunting complexity of Yeats's influences, pressures, ideas, and modes of persuasion that get in each other's way. Parts of it reinforce "crushingly conventional" patriarchal ideology, partly for its own presumed merits in fulfilling the speaker's responsibility and desire to "protect" his female child during a perilous time, but more pointedly for settling a score with a particular woman *and* opposing the ideas of a group of women whom the poet finds dangerous to his political and economic interests. In some sections, this ideology includes the self-congratulatory validation of an aristocracy over other classes. Other parts of it articulate a psychological perspective, inflected by theology and perhaps philosophy, that identifies the same transcendence of suffering and realization of individual contentment—reparation—that would be equally applicable to men and women, without hierarchy.

Those who believe that one particular set of concerns—whether (post)colonial or Marxist or gender-based or spiritually oriented—should be the central area of analysis and others must be peripheral (perhaps discardable) will find that reading contradictory impulses in Yeats's poem dilutes the interpretation and obscures what is most a construction and critique of the author's active and final intention. Others will insist upon elucidation of the contradictions and inconsistences in order to achieve fidelity to what they perceive as the complexity of authorial intention. If "A Prayer for My Daughter" is included as a choice for a research paper in a literature class, the professor's task can be to expose students to *some* differences of interpretation that I've discussed above, to figure out what would be too little, just right, and "too much information" (unlike what I have just done!). The professor would facilitate the class members' reflection on reasons for those differences and would begin to elicit their development of a reading in dialogue with secondary sources. If the poem is a choice for an essay that does not include research, the professor would need to find a way to streamline an account of differences among critics, even if some nuance had to be sacrificed.

So far, I have not discussed formal elements of Yeats's poem. Before doing so, I should mention the loose designation "New Formalism"—not to be confused with a coterie of US poets who, since the 1980s, have called for a return to traditional forms. Proponents of "New Formalism" have no intention of rehashing the "old formalism" of New Criticism. Fredric V. Bogel states that "New Formalisms ... critique and revise many of the theoretical assumptions of the New Criticism, including its conceptions of form and meaning, the ideas of intrinsic meaning and intrinsic literariness, 'organic' and other kinds of unity, the fiction of an 'ideal reader'" (9), etc. Susan J. Wolfson suggests that this "textual explication" of form "can attend to the several kinds of meanings that poetic form, both as a signifying performance and in its particular events, can enact in relation to ethical, historical, and social inquiry" (94). She perceives this kind of reading as engaging "what is most material in aesthetic practice." Bogel emphasizes New Formalist critics' "willingness to ally an unwavering methodological commitment" to concentrate on formal aspects of texts "with the diverse emphases, concerns, modes of analysis, and investments of a broad array of critical schools" (184). In my experience, few students have been interested in focusing on poetic form *unless* it can be related decisively to thematic components, and so the dual focus of the New Formalists seems promising for class discussion and essay development.

"A Prayer for My Daughter" includes some typical features of its period in Yeats's work. A New Formalist might say that these features exemplify the poet's historical situation: a transitional phase from patriarchal ideas to quasi-feminist concepts about equality. Yeats used traditional meter, rhyme, and stanza patterns, but his aesthetic imagination varies them to the point of "roughing them up." Each octave of "A Prayer" generally employs iambic pentameter in the first, second, third, fifth, and eighth lines and tetrameter in the fourth, sixth, and seventh, but in the final octave, the seventh line is in pentameter. Yet sometimes it is difficult to scan a line, when Yeats has more than one metrical substitution in a given octave. In the fifth stanza, for example, there is an initial spondaic substitution ("Hearts are") followed by a hypermetrical foot that creates an anapest ("as a gift") in the second line, as well as hypermetrical feet in the third and sixth lines and a hypometrical foot in the seventh, as well as an initial anapest in the final line. As for rhyme structure, Yeats, who writes a great deal in octaves, sometimes follows the *ottava rima* (abababcc) of Boccaccio, Ariosto, Tasso, and others, and at other times the scheme for the octave in the Petrarchan sonnet (abbaabba), but his departure in "A Prayer" is to use an aabbcddc rhyme, which moves the couplets of *ottava rima* to the first half and has twice as many, and in the second, uses the half of the repeated structure of the Petrarchan octave. Of equal importance to Yeats's innovations are the various slant rhymes—and I have found no evidence that he knew the work of Emily Dickinson—such as "dull"/"fool" (second octave), "man"/"undone" (third octave), "house"/"ceremonious" (eighth octave). The ambivalent use of traditional poetic devices might echo other kinds of ambivalence.

When I next teach "A Prayer for My Daughter," I will mention the relationship between the poem and the life of the actual Anne Butler Yeats. For students who choose to write about this text, this connection could be a more interesting focus for the conclusion than a rehashing of their thesis. Brenda Maddox, whose biography recounts numerous instances of the poet's marital infidelities, states that "stories of Yeats as a parent ... emphasize his distance from his children" and the judgment that he was "remote and preoccupied" (258). When Anne Yeats "laughed at the famous photograph of Yeats ... seated on the grass with a book at his feet and his two young children looking over his shoulder," she perceived "a man impatient to get back to his book." Maddox calls Anne's "predicament" in 1936 a reflection of "the protected status of girls of that time. Now seventeen, stage-struck, and gifted at theater design, she was expected to live at home, dependent on her parents, with no thought of higher education" (309), though her brother Michael, who like his father would become a senator, was given every educational advantage. "As her career progressed," Maddox continues, Yeats "fought hard against her spending too much time hanging about the Abbey and also opposed her wish (finally granted) to go to Paris to study. As he boasted to Ernest Rhys, ... 'Her sole education is languages, the Academy Art School and my conversation'" (310). Narrating a period roughly a year later, Maddox reports that letters between George and Yeats evinced their desire for "their daughter [to be] more stylish" (350). In a 1974 recording for the British Library National Sound Archive, Anne Yeats recalls that her father "scolded her if she went around with runs in her stockings and urged her to wear gold nail polish, and to dress exotically—like a character in one of his plays, she felt" (qtd in Maddox 350, n. 442). Maddox surmises that the couple were anxious that Anne "might not find the well-born husband who would 'bring her to a house/ Where all's accustomed, ceremonious.'" (350). Maddox reports that Anne, who stayed single, "said she found 'A Prayer for My Daughter' very hard to live up to."

Anne, who was almost twenty when her father died in January 1939, did not achieve one kind of "rootedness" that her father had in mind. However, in pursuing a professional life in the arts, Anne can be said to have acted in concert with Yeats's ideas about the soul's "self-delighting" "radical innocence." Ann Saddlemyer's article on her in *The Dictionary of Irish Biography* notes that "in 1936 at the age of 16 she was hired by the Abbey Theatre as an assistant to the chief designer," where "she designed the sets and costumes for" three "revivals of her father's plays," and "in 1939 she became head of design at the Abbey" while "also design[ing] and paint[ing] for the Abbey Experimental Theatre in the Peacock" ("Anne Butler Yeats") Theatre. Though Anne was fired from the Abbey in 1941 (see Saddlemyer, "Designing Ladies," 195–197) because of aesthetic differences with the management, she designed sets for various other theatres and an opera house, and gradually became "attracted more and more to painting as a career" ("Anne Butler Yeats") so she availed herself of further opportunities for study in the field. "In the 1950s, she began" to work as a book illustrator and designer, and during her painting career created site-specific "murals," co-founded "The Graphic Studio, where she worked on lithographs," taught art, and, with her brother, "reviv[ed] the Cuala Press" once run by her aunts. Her paintings were widely exhibited during her lifetime, and Ireland's National Gallery held "a memorial exhibition of twenty painting and drawings …" in June 2002. In no way a "flourishing hidden tree" immobilized "in one dear perpetual place" in the sense that Oates takes these phrases, Anne Yeats "was a member of the Irish delegation to China in 1956 and the Irish trade delegation to New York and Washington in 1963." She didn't enter political "thoroughfares" but was an active part of various artistic communities that contributed to the "ceremony" and "custom" of Irish culture, as her father and other family members did.

Julia Alvarez is best known as the author of the novels *How the Garcia Girls Lost Their Accents* and *In the Time of the Butterflies,* the story of sisters who were martyrs in the struggle against the Dominican Republic's dictator Trujillo. If Yeats in "A Prayer for My Daughter" is, in some sense, proposing psychological counseling in advance for his daughter Anne, Alvarez's poem "The Therapist" features a speaker on the receiving end of therapy. Straightforward descriptive and narrative elements make "The Therapist" a good candidate for surface reading. Stephen Best and Sharon Marcus, writing in 2009, group under the loose heading of "surface reading" what they consider "modes of reading that attend to the surfaces of texts rather than plumb their depths" (1–2). Best and Marcus "take surface to mean what is evident, perceptible, apprehensible in texts; what is neither hidden nor hiding," and they characterize it as "what insists on being looked *at* rather than what we must train ourselves to see *through*" (9). They assert that the reading of "*surface as literal meaning*" (12) can avoid the problem of blindness to salient facets of a text. In her study of "female friendship in Victorian novels," Marcus notes that critics have often read this topos "as a cover story for an otherwise unspeakable desire between women" and thus "have also assumed that courtship plots exile female friendship to the narrative margins." However, "Marcus shows female friends rarely lose their centrality in novels with marriage plots"; thus, "something true and visible on the text's surface" is what "symptomatic reading had ironically rendered invisible."

"The Therapist," like every poem in Alvarez's 2004 collection *The Woman I Kept to Myself*, features three stanzas of ten lines each. In French poetry of the Early Modern era, ten-line stanzas with ten syllables in each line are called *dizains*. Even though Alvarez minimally deviates from the syllable count, I think it is fair to call her stanzas by this name. Here is the poem:

He seems tired. (I'm his last appointment.)
Being wise all day probably takes its toll,
having to know but not appear to know
so patients search out answers on their own.
"Right?" I ask him. He shrugs, "If you say so."
"On the other hand:" he's fond of saying;
"You tell me what it means," he grins slyly—
transparent strategies, hoops I'll leap through
into happiness, if that's what it takes.
"Ah, happiness:" he sighs, again the grin.

Weekly, we meet. The clinic waiting room
Is strewn with cheap toys and old magazines
I never heard of: *Working Mother*, *Self*,
and one for kids with guessing games and jokes
none of them reads. One little girl tells me
her older brother's sick, "and mean," she adds.
Her frazzled mother scolds her, "Shut your mouth!"
lifting a threatening hand. "Sick!" she repeats
and bursts into giggles, and so do I.
I sober instantly when he appears.

We walk the endless hall. Along the way
the whirring noise machines outside each door
obscure confessions going on inside:
mothers who scold and swat, fathers who drink,
uncles who fondle, lovers who betray—
the whole sad gamut of inhumanity
we practice on each other, which is why
we've come here, sick and mean, to heal ourselves.
"Right?" I ask him. He's not supposed to say
what he knows, if he knows, what we're doing. (81)

A surface reading focuses on the concrete situation and does not look for "deep" meanings in the therapist's quoted remarks or his nonverbal communication. The patient shows empathy in the first two lines for the therapist. She is making excuses in advance for him in case his performance is not up to par. The first *dizain's* third and fourth lines directly state the patient's guesses about the therapist's method of treatment, and the rest of the stanza illustrates her sense of these "transparent strategies" through snippets of their dialogue, including her use of the abstraction "happiness" and his response that does not clarify anything further.

A surface reading notes that the second stanza temporarily leaves the interaction between patient and therapist and focuses on a description of the waiting room and the people in it. We learn that this environment includes typically inadequate distractions for both children and adults.

The speaker's discovery about a case of sibling rivalry and parental stress and impatience is just a typical example of how maladaptive family patterns would be revealed not only in a therapy session but right before it, as well as how kids can be disarmingly open with total strangers. The moment of solidarity between child and sympathetic adult eases the tension caused by the possibility that the mother, who may feel up to that point that the child is disturbing the speaker, will do more than "lift" the hand. However, this moment of quasi-levity is abruptly broken for the speaker when she is reminded of her visit's serious purpose.

The final *dizain*, which, unlike the previous ones, features a triple rhyme and an additional slant rhyme, continues in a descriptive mode, but the speaker is listing what she does not actually see yet thinks she has good reason to imagine. The quoted question in the second to last line makes the reader realize that this catalogue of imagined (in) human(e) interaction is actually a paraphrase of something that the speaker says to the therapist in order to get his response about the goal of treatment. She does not record an answer from him and leads us to believe that there is none, because she repeats her guess about his methodology stated at the beginning of the poem and adds that she is not sure "if he knows" what the therapy is supposed to accomplish or how they can achieve it. A surface reading, then, registers the patient's uncertainty about the purpose, significance, and likely outcome of the psychotherapeutic situation.

Alvarez's fiction tends to include a great deal of cultural allusion—such as references to how a family from the Dominican Republic negotiates the challenges of immigration to the United States in *How the Garcia Girls Lost Their Accents*, as well as specific images from the two cultures that appear in other poems in *The Woman I Kept to Myself*. However, "The Therapist" does not reveal the ethnicity or prior life-experience of the speaker or other characters. The only thing we know about the speaker is that she has elected to undergo treatment for psychological problems. Psychological discourse has much to say about clients' selective attention/perception, transference, and resistance. Within that discourse, those who oppose particular therapeutic theories and practices have strong views about misdiagnosis, inadequate or harmful treatment methods, and biased analysts/therapists. Some readers conversant with psychological theories will be inclined to consider the speaker an unreliable narrator and others a reliable one. The patient only represents the therapist's verbal and nonverbal communication in a handful of brief quotes and images, and these accompany her brief statements and conjectures about his motives. The poet does not present the therapist's own thinking or a substantial sampling of what he says to the client, so in something like a court of law, fair judgment of his character and job performance would be deemed unattainable. The narrator could be leaving out highly relevant components of his communication and her own because of memory lapses and resistance to sharing thoughts and feelings that she would find too painful or embarrassing or disempowering (in her attempt to gain an equal footing with him). The speaker doesn't tell us what problems she hopes to solve. We cannot judge her fairly, as we do not know whether she is reacting to a sincere, competent therapist or an indifferent, lazy, incompetent one. A surface reading doesn't fill in these gaps.

A reader might take the impossibility of a fully contextualized interpretation as a given and assume a particular vantage point—either one basically on the side of the speaker or on the side of the therapist—to see how this limited perspective enables her/him to derive a construction of active authorial intention or some amalgam of conscious and unconscious intention. (In this instance, unlike the case of Yeats's poem, there is no external evidence from interviews with Alvarez or other writings that the poem is biographical.) Among possible approaches, one can use deconstruction, not only to illustrate how gaps disable a single determinate interpretation, but to interrogate social hierarchies—for example, in a reading that values the claims of Alvarez's speaker over those of the therapist.

In Jacques Derrida's "*general strategy of deconstruction*" there is first "a phase of *overturning*"; as one apprehends the "violent hierarchy" of a binary opposition in which "one of the two terms governs the other ... or has the upper hand," s/he proceeds "to overturn the hierarchy at a given moment" (*Positions* 41). "Overturning" is also named "inversion" (42) or reversal. Derrida characterizes the second phase as "the irruptive emergence of a new 'concept'" that cannot exist within "the previous regime" (42). He gives various names to this non-concept (42–43); in English, this phase has frequently been translated as "displacement"; it dislodges the binary opposition. In "The Therapist," the immediate binary of therapist/patient soon evokes a set of associated binaries: knowledge/ignorance, competence/incompetence, independence/dependence, and authority/supplication. "Knowledge" involves the ability to discern psychological "meaning" and to "rescue" the "ignorant" patient from lack of meaning.

To think about how these binaries operate in the therapist–client interactions depicted by the poem's speaker, a reader must first rely to some extent on external evidence in the form of assumptions about the therapeutic context. One of these, I believe, is that a client, in signing up for therapy, accepts the therapist's authority, bolstered by a professional title based on educational achievement, and assumes that person will "be wise" in directing the course of treatment. In the third and fourth lines of "The Therapist," the speaker surmises that the therapist exerts authority to avoid coercion—to strengthen her independence so that she may find solutions to her own problems and have the possibility of arriving at competence, meaning, and knowledge that he already possesses. Yet her repeated desire for feedback shows that she appears uneasy and frustrated about how he authoritatively withholds knowledge. She wants reassurance that she understands the process, but she doesn't receive it. Also, the phrase, "on the other hand," unaccompanied by a clause that suggests what an ostensibly better alternative could be, suggests that the client feels dependent on the psychologist's contributions to the dialogue, but his authoritative implications of negative interpretation are not accompanied by clues that might lead to her "correct" responses.

In the opening lines, it is unclear whether the client is actually telling the therapist (rather than thinking) that he appears "tired." If she directly communicates this to him, then she is getting personal, and he may believe that she is looking for his vulnerability in order to "become friends," which would undermine his professional posture of neutrality. Many Freudians and some practitioners with other orientations consider their neutrality a necessary measure to enable patients to "search out answers" without distraction. (An instructor may need to make students aware of this bit of *possible* external evidence.) In performing neutrality, the therapist would not admit that he is feeling tired; he exercises the authority not to direct attention to himself. When the speaker asks him to confirm her hypothesis stated in the first four lines, his noncommittal shrug and perfunctory statement shifting interpretive responsibility to her signals his refusal to disclose his methodology. This may be to promote her independent search for answers, but it could also be to preserve his authority to control the flow of the treatment against her resistance. From this perspective, "You tell me what it means" is structured as a command, not merely an invitation. The therapist's ambiguous "grins" are especially authoritative, since they could be an ironic dismissal of what the patient has just said. The phrase "Ah, happiness" and accompanying sigh might be read as mocking the patient for her "naïve" use of language or wistfully gesturing to the impossibility of reaching such a goal. This ambiguous communication keeps the client off balance, which may not facilitate but *hinder* her search. Also, in denying her a precise sense of his objectives, the therapist reduces his accountability while providing no hope that the client's suffering will end. If she continues to have faith in his institutionally sanctioned credentials, it could prolong and intensify her desperation to find elusive meaning that is supposed to improve the trajectory of her life-narrative—which in turn could make her even more dependent on his alleged knowledge and ability. Thus, his actions may reinforce rather than lessen the speaker's sense of incompetence and ignorance.

The exposure of what makes this relationship asymmetrical can permit a reader to locate a deconstructive reversal of the hierarchy of these binary oppositions. The reader (and perhaps the client) is aware of the therapist's manipulation of the dialogic situation and thus can find meanings that the psychologist would conceal—including *his* dependence on her uncertainty about his modus operandi and her compliance with how he orchestrates their patterns of communication. And without clients, he can't earn a living at his chosen profession. A dissatisfied patient who has not been placed in therapy by the legal system has the power to end the sessions at any time. Some details in the second *dizain* might also illuminate the questionable nature of a posited authority and presumed knowledge that depends on the insecurity of those who accept the label "sick" (or even "mean") for themselves. For example, the magazine *Working Mother* may instruct a "frazzled" working mother about how to manage her life in ways that serve consumer culture rather than her autonomy, and the magazine *Self* may "inform" someone with a fragile sense of identity how to engage in self-construction through material consumption rather than careful self-examination. The "frazzled mother's" threat of physical violence against her "little girl" signals that the authority to compel another to refrain from self-expression is arbitrary; one might consider it the flip side of the therapist's command to the speaker to produce meaning. Perhaps the little girl and the speaker use "giggles" to reverse the hierarchy, at least momentarily. If this environment dictates that one must be a "sober" participant who delivers "obscure [therapeutic] confessions" and does not converse with strangers, bursts of "drunken" irreverence expose the shaky foundations and functioning of the binary of authority figure/supplicant.

Finding that both the therapist and client can exert authority (for instance, over meaning), display a kind of competence, and exhibit independence and dependence in different ways, a deconstructive reader perceives the inability of the binary oppositions to authorize a particular hierarchy. This is displacement, Derrida's second phase of deconstruction. In the difference between the third line, indicating what the speaker *must* know while seeming not to, and the final sentence, which includes the conditional, "if he knows," it is possible to discern progress from a possible relative acceptance of the original hierarchy near the beginning to reversal and displacement at the end of the poem. The speaker no longer states that the therapist *must* know "answers" that will accomplish psychological healing of the "sick and mean"; she entertains the possibility that his "transparent" or elusive strategies camouflage his lack of knowledge/wisdom and the questionable aspects of institutional credentials. He may *never* reply in the affirmative to her "right?" but could endlessly postpone any substantive interpretive gesture. This realization of uncertainty may not bring the reparation that the speaker wants, but it could involve partial reparation: the reduction of self-blame and hence anxiety about "walk[ing] the [seemingly] endless hall" of therapy and the possibility of walking away from unsatisfactory sessions and trying other ways of "healing" herself. This perspective on "The Therapist" (a poem which is *not* titled "Therapy") involves a critique of general or particular practices and evasions of some therapists and the institutions that they represent. Readers can reflect on whether they think the poem exposes *potential* problems in therapy/analysis in general, or whether it supports the idea that these problems are so widespread that "talk therapy" is basically useless.

Let us now consider a psychological reading that validates the therapist's conduct and finds that the patient causes problems for herself. In this scenario, Alvarez is consciously or unconsciously deploying dramatic irony; there are reasons for readers not to identify with the speaker's thinking and perhaps to relate it to their own past errors. One can assume that the speaker in the first *dizain* has empathy for the therapist's probable weariness or that she takes an opportunity to get the upper hand in a situation where she otherwise feels a lack of agency. In both cases, the reader believes that the patient has guessed correctly about the therapist's methodology and that his effort to get her to seek her own solutions is a legitimate strategy, whether "transparent" or not. When she seeks validation ("Right?") for her statements at every turn, she undermines this agenda; it would serve the treatment much better if she complied with his benevolent authority by patiently exploring what is "on the other hand" and by allowing meaning to unfold slowly rather than acting impatiently. Also, the vagueness of the speaker's use of such abstract words as "happiness" works against the eventual development of concrete goals and specific paths toward achieving them, so the therapist's evasive response is justified, and his "grins" aren't read as sarcastic.

For the most part, the pro-therapist interpretation of the second *dizain* and the first half of the third corresponds to that of the surface reading, except that this imagery and narration pave the way for the speaker's grand generalization in the final stanza's second half about "the ... gamut of inhumanity" that people inflict on one another. The reader could see this as an absurdly sweeping remark about "the human condition" of "sickness" and "meanness" or an ironic jab at what she inaccurately sees as the judgmental, supercilious attitude of therapists who treat them. Either way, the utterance ignores either the variety of specific problems that bring people into therapy or the different forms of treatment and attitudes of therapists. The patient's final "'Right?'" could be a conscious attempt or unconscious impulse to goad her therapist into an admission that people's problems are so immense that the therapeutic enterprise is hopelessly inadequate in enabling them to "heal themselves." If it is a way of goading him into providing a more specific, elaborate justification for her investment in their sessions, the therapist senses that any justification he might try would provoke more questions and divert the client from doing the hard work of tackling the roots of her difficulties.

Investment of time and money in psychotherapy is always a gamble, since the acquisition of insight that will transform one's emotional life is never a given, but the poem's speaker lets her ambivalence about taking the gamble loom large. (This ambivalence may be mirrored in Alvarez's meter: I count one nine-syllable line [the first], two eleven syllable lines [the second and twenty-fourth], thirteen lines of "perfect" iambic pentameter, and fourteen other ten-syllable lines, some of which are essentially iambic pentameter with one metrical substitution and others of which are far from iambic.) "If he knows," the dependent clause tucked into the middle of the last line, suggests resistance. Although this parting shot in the temporally limited poem does not necessarily indicate the cessation of their therapy, the patient casts doubt on both the potential of treatment and the therapist's behavior, as though he is contributing to the immense "quantity" of "inhumanity" by performing his job in bad faith. She does not trust the therapist enough to go along unreservedly with his "transparent strategies, hoops," so she sabotages the process. A pro-therapy and pro-therapist reader, in judging the speaker to be an unreliable narrator, finds her fragmentary presentation of evidence about the therapist's part of their interactions evidence that she is so preoccupied with his "evasions" that she doesn't even listen to, much less record his most useful remarks. And if she were able to listen and absorb these interventions, she might be able to make a fuller commitment to the therapy for whatever time would be needed to effect positive change.

Both the deconstructive and pro-therapist psychological readings of "The Therapist" depend heavily on the positing of external evidence that Alvarez may or may not have considered. They rely on "mind-reading" of the two principals based on application of knowledge about psychological theories, common sense notions of human behavior, and awareness of conventions of psychotherapy/analysis. Especially compared to the relative thinness of the surface reading, I don't see this as a problem: grappling with these two takes on the poem's representation of the therapeutic event can generate salient critical thought about notions of communication, individual psychological development, and power relations.

A.K. Ramanujan's poem "Death and the Good Citizen" (1986) articulates three different views about what should be done with a dead body. The first of these, which takes up a little more than half of the poem, involves the notion of recycling. However, the first of four, fifteen-line free verse stanzas does not begin to approach the theme of death announced by the title. Ramanujan's speaker addresses a "good citizen" whose city "by special arrangement" collects its people's "nightsoil" while it is "still/ warm every morning/ in a government/ lorry, drippy (you said)/ ... to the municipal gardens," and his vivid imagery shows how useful the recycled shit becomes:

... to make the grass
  grow tall for the cows
in the village, the rhino
  in the zoo: and the oranges
plump and glow, till
  they are a preternatural
orange. (135)

At the beginning of the second stanza, Ramanujan's speaker confers the titles of "good animal, yet perfect/ citizen" on his addressee, because, unlike those who will "decompose" rather than be "dismantled," s/he sanctions her/his postmortem recycling: "you, you are/ biodegradable, you do/ return to nature: you will/ your body to the nearest/ hospital, changing death into small/ change and spare parts ..." (135). The pun on "change" is especially felicitous, because the unity of the individual in death is transformed and divided into items that will serve as currency for various purposes. The substitution of a condition (the state of "death") for an object (the corpse) that exhibits the state is the first in a series of metonyms that, along with the poet's use of personification, will be important to conflicting ideas about the poet's active intentions in this meditative lyric.

Ramanujan's description of his first of two examples demonstrates how practical yet unsettling this recycling is:

    Eyes in an eye bank
  to blink some day for a stranger's
    brain, wait like mummy wheat
in the singular company
  of single eyes, pickled,
absolute. (135)

The noun "bank," continuing the drift implied by the pun on "change," stresses the socioeconomic value of the "good citizen's" bequest. But the idea of the eyes "blinking" in a "stranger's" head on behalf of that person's "brain" (rather than the simple notion of someone giving sight to someone else) makes the transplant seem bizarre, perhaps unnatural, though elements of nature are being exchanged. The enjambment separating "stranger's" and "brain" emphasizes this strange dislocation and relocation, as does the personification of the main subject "eyes" connected grammatically to the main verb "wait" two lines later. Beneficiaries of the "eyes" wait, while dead people and their organs do not. Such personification spookily converts material with potential to serve the living into a living "being." And the simile of "mummy wheat," a trope used more than once by W.B. Yeats, signifies the supposedly miraculous preservation of an ancient Egyptian harvest. It also conveys the repeated "singularity" of individual eyes, separated from their partners and saved from decay by being "pickled." The tropes suggest an ambivalence about this "recycling."

Hailing from Mysore, India, Ramanujan (1929–93), a folklorist, philologist, and translator as well as a poet in both English and his native Kannada, came to the United States and spent his last three decades as a professor in several departments at the University of Chicago. He has been hailed as a postcolonial literary figure. In a reading of "Death and the Good Citizen," Jahan Ramazani detects a "postcolonial impetus behind Ramanujan's multilayered meditation on the recirculation of nutrients, organs and texts" involving "cultural displacement and integration" (94–95). He emphasizes the poet's depiction of the ironic, sometimes sinister aspects of postmortem "redistribution" rather than the ecologically salubrious ones. He refers to the apostrophe to the "good citizen" as conveying "mock" rather than genuine "admiration" and surmises that this figure "conceives of himself in terms of his elements, in metaphors of bodily dispersal, translation, and displacement" (93). Ramazani regards "the citizen's life [as] a daily diaspora, a scattering of himself into other lives and places"; he perceives the "disembodied" organs of deceased people that "are deposited in 'banks,'" where "they form an amusingly anonymous company of sorts," not only as "isolated" but as "decontextualized" (94), rather than on the way to a useful *re*contextualization. Drawing no explicit distinction between a living being and a corpse in this "literary version of postcolonial reincarnation," he considers "the citizen" to be "erod[ing] the finality of the boundary against which the self normally constitutes its uniqueness" through a conception of "the self as an assembly of discrete parts that might function within other human structures."

In the first part of the poem's third stanza, while addressing how the transplant of a deceased person's organ requires the adaptation of the beneficiary's body, the speaker uses the second example of organ recycling either to praise the donor's laudable temperament, as though this would facilitate success, or, in Ramazani's view, to offer him/her mock praise:

> Hearts,
>   with your kind of temper,
>   may even take, make connection
> with alien veins, and continue
>   your struggle to be naturalized:
> beat, and learn to miss a beat
>   in a foreign body. (136)

The "magic" of personification can't really make a dead person continue to care about matters of non-native citizenship, assimilation, and retention of native culture. However, the contrast between the noun "connection" and the adjectives "alien" and "foreign," as well as the political connotations of those adjectives and the "struggle to be naturalized," supports Ramazani's postcolonial reading: "Disorienting and incongruous, the postcolonial or diasporic experience resembles the ultimate crossing of boundaries—between one body and another. Ramanujan's exhilarating metaphorical leap from interbodily to intercultural transplantation suggests how precarious, violent, and strange it is to be retrofitted into a new national and social organization" (95). The transplanted eye or heart may have trouble adapting "to its new surroundings," yet "the poem implicitly invites our hearts to 'take, make connection/ with alien veins,' with the individual sensibility and cultural experience inscribed within its lines."

In the rest of the third stanza, Ramanujan's speaker, born Hindu in India like the poet himself, provides a second perspective on how to treat the body after death. Calling his "tribe, incarnate/ unbelievers in bodies," he asserts that his Hindu family will "speak proverbs, contest/ my will, against such degradation" (136) if he dies in his native land. The speaker perceives the Hindu ritual of cremation as a "sterilization" of the individual—likely an elimination of the body's interference with the soul's successful reincarnation: "Hidebound, even worms cannot/ have me: they'll cremate/ me in Sanskrit and sandalwood,/ have me sterilized/ to a scatter of ash." The repetition of "have me" reinforces the anticipated imposition of "hidebound" tradition on the speaker "against [his] will"—in both senses of "will." It is possible that the speaker would prefer to follow the postmortem wishes of "the good citizen," even if it parallels the disquieting series of postcolonial displacements.

A little more than half of the fourth and final stanza concerns itself with burial, the third and final way of managing the corpse. Ramazani sees both "Hindu cremation and American embalming" as "efforts ... to defeat physical recirculation" (95) and believes that "Ramanujan makes the burial practices of his Western readers look even more absurd" than "the crematory practices of his Indian readers" (96). Indeed, the poet's representation of US funeral home practices is full of irony:

> Or abroad,
> they'll lay me out in a funeral
>   parlour, embalm me in pesticide,
> bury me in a steel trap, lock
>   me out of nature
> till I'm oxidized by left-
>   over air, withered by my own
> vapours into grin and bone. (136)

The use of the noun "pesticide" as a substitute for embalming fluid underscores that both insects and corpses are nuisances to agricultural professionals and morticians who serve Judeo-Christian customers. Ironically, the kinds of chemicals that kill insects are needed for a corpse's temporary, unnatural preservation before it can be allowed to be "oxidized" and "vaporized." The reference of the pronoun "me" to the (future) corpse continues the poem's deployment of personification, as though this confinement "in a steel trap" is an indignity to the "prisoner" "who" should at least be allowed to merge with the earth. This dead body would not suffer from being "trapped"; the consequence is that its parts could not benefit the living. Ramazani points out that the poet's allusion to Yeats's "Sailing to Byzantium" in "lock/ me out of nature" recalls "Yeats's mildly ironized hope of transcending nature through art, counterpointing it with humanity's pathetic attempts at escape through burial and crematory practices" (96). The ghoulish metonym of "grin," the fiction of an animate human being within the inanimate, as a substitute for the lower part of the skull reveals that the bare final residue, though hidden, will still exist "in nature"—uselessly. "Death and the Good Citizen" concludes:

> My tissue will never graft,
> will never know newsprint,
>   never grow in a culture,
>   or be mould and compost
>   for jasmine, eggplant
> and the unearthly perfection
>   of municipal oranges. (136)

According to Ramazani, Ramanujan's suggestive image of "newsprint" and his pun on "culture" seemingly "suggest that" embalming and cremation "aim for a purity translatable into xenophobia," yet the poet's "metamorphosing the English language, Western lyric tropes, the Anglo-Irish Yeats, Hindu ritual, even his own words in this poem" constitutes a warning "that the quest for inviolable closure in death risks cultural sterility and claustrophobia" (96). He underscores the poet's realization, applicable to "individuals, poems, and cultures," that "endings" are uncontrollable and "are openings into new worlds, new metamorphoses." On the other hand, Vinay Dharwadker, in his Introduction to Ramanujan's *Collected Poems*, finds the speaker's parting shot an ironic recognition that nature always absorbs a corpse; the universal effect of death and inevitable disintegration of all matter "finally" undermines the relevance of sociocultural differences in the ways the living manage a dead body.

A reader might assess the relevance of the poem's staging of conflict among the three postmortem practices somewhat differently than either Dharwadker or Ramazani does. "Death and the Good Citizen" was first published in *Poetry* magazine in 1981, a time when international concerns about environmental degradation, especially pollution, were far from new. (Half a century ago, both the U.S. Environmental Protection Agency—due to a bipartisan consensus sanctioned by President Richard Nixon—and Earth Day were established.) According to an article in the *Smithsonian Magazine*, "the environmental movement of the 1970s can be credited with directly shaping American recycling programs—although concern about the post-war disposable culture goes back almost to its beginning" (Eschner). An interpreter examining the poem through the lens of ecocriticism would either challenge Ramazani's assumption that the speaker is merely *pretending* to praise the "good citizen" and Dharwadker's sense that the ending reflects how the choice of "disposal" is ultimately inconsequential, or else would assert that either the author's active (and perhaps final) intention or his unconscious intention exceeds the speaker's apparent perspective. In such a reading, both internal evidence and external (historical) evidence would point to an affirmation of pragmatic use of resources and an ironic critique of outmoded practices that prove wasteful and even toxic.

According to the ecocritical reading, even if excremental discourse is a staple of comedy, the "nightsoil" initiative beginning the poem is neither silly nor trivial. The extremely lyrical ending and the fact that the "oranges" are labeled "municipal" indicates that this kind of "urban planning," however odd, can have excellent effects. "Unearthly perfection," recalling the first stanza's "preternatural orange," may be hyperbolic, but passages in the first two-and-a-half stanzas decisively present the benefits of repurposing/recycling. And when Ramazani speaks of the citizen's self-conception of bodily fragmentation and self-scattering (93), couldn't this be considered a problematic synecdochic association between the citizen's identity and his/her waste product, as though the character would have any possibility of not "dispersing" or "displacing" it somewhere or harbor any desire to hold onto it as a "valuable" mark of identity? Unlike the postcolonial situation of whether one remains in one's country or emigrates, shit only gains value when "dispersed" in ways like those the poem mentions. Making a personal contribution to a sustainable ecological practice as part of a municipal effort is not tantamount to suffering an identitarian crisis due to postcolonial displacement.

Organ repurposing can improve the quality of (other) people's lives, and both cremation and embalming have environmental drawbacks and do not come with the first option's advantages. For Ramazani, the poet critiques cremation and embalming because of their attempt to create illusory boundaries, and he bases his sense of the relative validity of organ donation on a concept that he finds congruent with postcolonial actuality: the realization conveyed in the poem that "neither the beginnings nor the endpoints of the self are singular and fixed" but rather "fluid, manifold, and indeterminate" (93). He neither denies nor underscores the ecological possibilities of this point.

An ecocritical reading could examine effects produced when Ramanujan repeatedly plays with the idea that the dead body and its parts continue their union with the same human identity that the (former) possessor of a functioning brain and heart had. Metonymy, synecdoche, personification, or prosopopeia (the dead having a "face" or "speaking"), which enable this kind of gesture in poetry, obscure the idea that eyes and heart are of no use to someone after death. The difference between the implication that the corpse's parts remain the property or continue to be integral to the (non-)being of an individual's unified self and a concept negating this implication may prove the crux of the dispute between certain theological positions and an ecocritical stance. Alternatively, a reader might decide that this poem reflects Ramanujan's active and/or final intention *not* to support a particular view, but just to include material for a postcolonial reading, an ecocritical one, and perhaps others.

In her 2011 poem "(mis)takes one to know one," Evie Shockley utilizes the dream appearance of Frederick Douglass as a touchstone of liberation in order to dramatize uncertainty about ideological assessment of President Barack Obama's commitment to African-Americans after two years in office. The title of Shockley's book, *The New Black* (2011), plays on "the New Negro" of the Harlem Renaissance, as well as fashion industry fickleness. According to James Brunton, "the title ... gestures toward a notion of blackness in a new context—specifically, that of America during the Obama administration," and the allusion to fashion "casts a note of irony over this claim of newness. The title asks us to consider the absurd claim that the United States has entered a new post-racial future with the election of a black President" (69). In fact, the first poem in the book begins: "a clean-cut man brings a brown blackness/ to a dream-carved, unprecedented/place. some see this as the end of race ..." (1). The punning on "race" and other words that follow this opening gambit shows that one should reject the claim.

College students who read "(mis)takes one to know one" from this point forward may have been in high school or junior high when Obama left office; many may not have been aware that left African-American intellectuals like Michael Eric Dyson, Melissa Harris-Perry, Ta-Nehisi Coates, and, most pointedly, Cornel West have registered sharp criticisms of Obama's record on issues pertaining to Black people. Therefore, aside from making allusion to Frederick Douglass, an important part of the external evidence needed to interpret the poem, an instructor should help students understand the president's own representation of his intentions and the context of *varying* African-American perceptions of Obama.

In the first installment of his presidential autobiography, *A Promised Land* (2020), Obama speaks of the context of race in his 2008 campaign strategy. He contextualizes the most broadly remembered part of the speech at the 2004 Democratic National Convention that brought him into prominence, "'There is not a Black America and a white America and a Latino America and an Asian America. There's the *United States of America*,'" by describing it "more as a statement of aspiration than a description of reality," yet something he "strove for" (114–115). Obama asserts his commitment to prioritizing "our common humanity" over "our differences," and he considers it a matter of practicality, since "big change" in the United States could only be achieved if he resorted to "building coalitions across racial and ethnic lines" (115). Declaring that he hoped to place "issues like inequality ... at the very center of the debate and then actually deliver the goods" (118) through a broad coalition, Obama realizes: "It was a lot to ask of Black folks, requiring a mixture of optimism and strategic patience" (119). Obama speaks of "activists and intellectuals who supported [him]" in 2008 as a symbol who could "raise a prophetic voice against racial injustice" with the understanding that he could not win the general election, and they wanted the candidate to take "uncompromising positions on everything from affirmative action to reparations ..." (117). For these activists, "courting ... less progressive white folks" was not acceptable.

Dyson, Harris-Perry, and Coates temper their critiques by mentioning factors that made it extremely difficult for President Obama: the hullabaloo over his birth certificate, Tea Party rage over the moderate president's "communist" initiatives like universal health care, and ceaseless obstruction by Congressional Republicans of his calm attempts to reach consensus. Dyson declares that "Obama missed a boatload of opportunities to deal with the issue of race" because he wished to keep "his poll numbers" high and because "he figured that his very presence would evoke enough consciousness about race"; the president thought that "he could use the bully pulpit sparingly" when "the issues ... force themselves upon him ..." Dyson surmises that Obama "didn't want to be ghettoized," "to be seen as the black president," but argues that Obama should see himself as "the president of black Americans," who deserved equality under law. Further, the fact that African-Americans in general were reluctant "to criticize Obama at all because he was the first black president" and "he knew it" facilitated what Dyson calls his "racial procrastination."

Since 2009 and steadily up until today, Cornel West has excoriated Obama's record. First, he castigates the 44th president's handling of the financial crisis inherited from the second Bush administration: He numbers himself among those "few" who "begged and pleaded with Obama to break with the Wall Street priorities and bail out Main Street," whereas the President "bail[ed] out Wall Street" ("Pity the Sad Legacy of Barack Obama") and protected the perpetrators. West also links the failure to punish "US torturers of innocent Muslims" and to protest the Israeli army's killing of numerous Palestinians with a neglect of African-Americans. In 2012, he ties the "catastrophic situation" of "the black poor and working class," including "Depression levels of unemployment and underemployment," "dilapidated housing and disgraceful school systems," "guns and drugs and in the community, devastated lives and too many people dead" ("President Obama and the Crisis of Black America") to Obama's domestic record. West also cited increased incidents of police brutality against African-Americans that led (after Shockley's poem was written) to the Black Lives Matter movement.

With some background, students who had only been aware of Obama's struggles with right-wing forces can appreciate how ideological interpretation is at stake in "(mis)takes one to know one." The poem's unitalicized speaker, who is given a very few sentences, begins by declaring: "i dreamed i told frederick douglass/ barack obama isn't black, not yet!" (80). The speaker displaces one kind of metonymic thinking with another: a person's racial identity, conventionally identified by ancestral lineage, is now judged by mindset/action. Douglass (whose voice is in italics) immediately responds to the speaker with fierce intensity:

> the gray elder statesman, in the shape
>   he assumes for oneiric work, he gave
> me the look that covey surely took
>   with him to his grave: direct metal
> to match the channel carved between
>   his brows, the cheekbones driving
> up toward decision-making. *the child*
>   *follows the condition of the mother? don't*

mix up servitude and race. i would think
the president of the united states could
not be a slave to anyone or anything
except his own desires. (80)

The "oneiric" Douglass's opening rhetorical question challenges a reversal of the racist "one-drop rule," as though the fact of Obama's white mother "dilutes" or even disables his paternal claim to African heritage. After the "direct metal" "look" that he bestowed upon the sadistic slave-tamer Covey, Douglass's aim as an abolitionist is precisely to separate "servitude and race." He does not believe that the president must exist in "servitude" to a US history of white-dominant politics but can only be undermined by intense craving that sabotages more constructive aims. At this point, with awareness of external evidence, a twenty-first-century reader such as the dreamer could doubt the dream-Douglass's reliability, as he is compromised by his nineteenth-century perspective and overemphasizes a president's power in modern times. He can't see how corporate and political organizations and individuals that enable the modern "chief executive" to have enough campaign funds to win the White House exert greater pressure than these forces did on presidents from Lincoln through Cleveland. And the long-standing failure of the US Congress to enact meaningful campaign finance reform means that members of the legislative branch are also affected by the influence of individual and corporate donors who may pressure them not to support presidential initiatives. Further, the judicial branch can sometimes restrict the president's ability to lead, to fulfill "desires." Douglass continues:

but black? answer
this: what is the story your president tells
of his life? that is the question. always,
some among us have chosen to be or
not to be what laws or customs inscribe
in our blood. race is not biology: it is
the way the wind blows when you enter
a room, how you weather the storms,

how you handle being becalmed. black,
       white, red—colors, symbols, myths. i
             never knew a white parent to stand
    between a colored man and his destiny. (80)

Aside from the convention speech, Barack Obama rose to public attention because of "the story [he] tells of his life": *Dreams from My Father*, the autobiography in which he explains how his "white parent" did not "stand/ between" him as "a colored man and his destiny," as Frederick Douglass's white father did not. Obama explains how he came to identify himself in Chicago with the African part of his familial inheritance and to become a community organizer to empower an African-American constituency. Although that context is not available to the oneiric Douglass, as it is to the dreamer, readers can take what he says about the *choice* of identification—echoing Hamlet's most famous soliloquy—and subsequent action resisting the "inscription" of "laws or customs" as pertinent to a recognition of Obama's active solidarity with African-Americans *before* his presidential quest.

Douglass's maxim, "race is not biology," which jibes with the current concept of "social constructivism," entails debunking of "symbols, myths" attached to racial categorization. The passage that freshens the old trope of "the wind" by placing it in "a room" can be related to the trouble Obama faced when he "enter[ed the] room" of a national campaign and then the Oval Office. The question for the poem's speaker is whether Obama is "weather[ing] the storms" of his presidency and "handl[ing] being becalmed" in ways that support improving conditions for African-Americans.

In most of the second strophe, Douglass emphasizes the extent of change that he saw in his lifetime. In doing so, "he rebutted [the] cocked eye-/ brow" (80) of the speaker, who may sense that the formative influence of European-American culture on Obama, albeit amid Hawaii's diversity, prompts him to sacrifice African-American communities' crucial objectives in order to maintain a multi-racial, multi-ethnic coalition and make incremental progress toward social justice. Douglass relives his amazement that, in the Civil War,

> *white men*
> *would kill white men by the hundreds*
> *of thousands freeing the negro—even as*
> *the desperate, calculated means to purely*
> *economic ends.* exhaling outrageously,
> he adjusted the vest around his barrel
> chest and relaxing waistline. *but war*
> *came and, in its wake, amendments—*
> *if not amends—were made.* (81)

Are the speaker's stage directions interrupting the flow of Douglass's statement merely descriptions that humanize a noble figure, or do the phrases "exhaling outrageously" and "relaxing waistline" slightly mock a performance designed to counter the speaker's pessimism? Or could the stage direction be read as Shockley's deliberate ambiguity of tone? The actual Douglass is a reliable narrator of his time, but the dream is putting him in the tough position of thinking about a future on the basis of events he has experienced. In any case, his distinction between "amendments" and "amends" indicates the severely limited progress made during Reconstruction.

Next, Douglass points out that he was the vice presidential candidate on "*the equal rights/ ticket*" only "seven years after [the Civil War's] end" (81). However, there is a significant irony in this admission: "Douglass never appeared at the party's nominating convention, never agreed to run with Woodhull," the Equal Rights Party's presidential candidate, "never participated in the campaign and actually gave stump speeches for Grant" (Felsenthal), who won re-election to a second term. (Other ironies are that Victoria Woodhull would have been 34 on inauguration day in 1873 and therefore ineligible for the office, and she could not vote in the election, as women gained the franchise in 1920.) Without the benefit of this external evidence, a reader would take the oneiric Douglass's information as reason to view it a sign of actual progress rather than a sign of the caginess with which the poet seems to have imbued him: "*no, the equal rights/ ticket didn't win, and it only took/ another one hundred and thirty-six years/ to put a colored man in the white house*." "Only?" The abolition of slavery was achieved "only" 246 years after the importation of slaves to North America in 1619. It is hard to determine the extent to which Douglass counsels his listener to find encouragement in American history.

The final lines indicate that Douglass will not end the dream/poem with optimism *or* pessimism: "*your president will be what/ his country has taught him to be, will/ do what his experience leads him to do./ don't mix up change with progress*" (81). Since the poem's speaker does not supply it, an interpreter of "(mis)takes one to know one" must utilize nothing but external evidence to speculate on what the United States "has taught" Obama to be and what facets of "his experience" are most influential in "leading" his actions during roughly the first half of his first term in the White House. I can hypothesize that Obama was constrained by the neoliberal turn in electoral politics occasioned by the "Reagan Revolution," which thwarted gains of sixties left movements and slowed the pace of African-American empowerment. "Racial procrastination" might be traced to the impact of Obama's inheritance of the financial crisis, pressure to affirm the necessity of a corporate bailout (which West decries) to jumpstart the economy, the Tea Party's virulent, frequently racialized attacks, a general lack of cooperation from Republicans in Congress, and the strain of trying to handle crisis after crisis, foreign and domestic, while ironing out all the compromises and dilution that led to the passage of the Affordable Care Act in 2010. Inextricable from all of these aspects, fully detailed in *A Promised Land*, was the need to figure out how to maintain his base and win reelection, as Obama proved able to do in 2012.

The word "change," along with the phrase "yes, we can," was crucial to Obama's 2008 campaigns against Clinton and McCain (and by extension, George W. Bush). By putting the distinction between "change" and "progress" in the dream Douglass's mouth as a parting shot, a reader might assume that Shockley actively or finally intends to say that Obama is not "Black." Like West and Dyson, she might hold him responsible for policies that have not amounted to "progress" for African-Americans or the country at large, even if there is a "change" from the previous administration. The "not yet" at the beginning of the poem holds out the possibility that Obama can achieve "progress" in a second term, something which his aforementioned Black critics on the left assert didn't happen. However, another interpreter could counter that the speaker does not respond to Douglass's final remarks, which draw no conclusion about Obama's "blackness," so Shockley finally intends to place the burden of judgment on Black readers' examination of external evidence. And perhaps the parentheses in the poem's title suggest an uncertainty that suspends decision: it may "take" an African-American "to know" another African-American's identity or the former can be mistaken about the latter.

Evaluation, I surmise, hinges on the question of whether the shortcomings attributed to Obama's record by West and Dyson are due primarily to the president's errors in policy formation and action *or* to external problems that severely limit his efficacy, and also on the weighing Obama's accomplishments, acknowledged by Dyson and some other left Black intellectuals, against his failures. The poem itself covers a short time span, and one may also ask whether it is reasonable to expect quick progress, especially directly after a major financial crisis.

Analysis of Shockley's text based on a great deal of external evidence does not mean that the poem is merely a jumping off point for a political science or history topic. A class's close attention to the text's internal evidence, including tropes, and gaps in evidence, as well as the elusiveness of some of the dream-Douglass's pronouncements, should take up much time and energy *before* students reach the stage of trying to develop a conjecture about Shockley's political stance or suspension of one.

In his poetry, Timothy Liu, who does not discourage readers from identifying many of his speakers with himself, frequently represents sexual acts and attitudes that can be interpreted as transgressive—vigorously defying homophobia, heterosexism, and religious prohibition—*or* as confessional, revealing vulnerabilities and other uncertainties. It is also possible to find that both tendencies are operative. The transgression/confessional binary can be linked with differences between two strategies designed to empower gay (but also LGBTQIA) communities. Writing in 2011 about the concept of a "post-gay era" emerging around the turn of the millennium, Amin Ghaziani notes an oscillation "over the long course of gay history, but especially from 1950s homophile organizing onward ... between" a strategy of "assimilation," "a narrow, single-interest vision, rooted in conventional identity politics, that seeks an end to discrimination against gays, and" a focus on "diversity," "an expansive, multi-issue, coalition view that is grounded in a political philosophy of intersectionality and social justice" (103). Those gay activists, such as those in the movement for marriage equality, who support assimilation seek to overcome the limitations of "urban ghettoization" and achieve socioeconomic advantages through "enter[ing] the public sphere," whereas "diversity" activists believe that "assimilation is socially homogenizing and erases a unique gay sensibility" and leaves a fundamental heterosexism intact. Ghaziani suggests that "post-gay" could develop into "a multicultural blurring of modernist boundaries and a move toward expanded tolerance and freedom—or it could entail a neoliberal, class- and racially inflected, and surface blurring that redefines the contours of hetero- and homonormativity" (120).

The title of Timothy Liu's poem "The Prodigal Son Writes Home" (1998) features an interesting ambiguity. The speaker literally writes to his father's address, which might be the actual home from which he has "prodigally" strayed, and he speaks extremely directly about his behavior. The poem narrates a refusal to return home to the father's values, as in the original Christian tale in the book of Luke of the prodigal son. Especially in the poem's first half, exhibitionism in writing can signify further rebellion, a violation not only of the parent's likely belief in what Adrienne Rich has called "compulsory heterosexuality," but of his overall sense of "decency"—including separation of sexual practices and other bodily functions. It may well involve ironic pleasure in the sudden power that he exerts over a (former?) authority figure:

I want to tell you how he eats my ass
even in public places, Father dear,
the elastic round my waist his finger hooks
as it eases down my crack (no classified
ad our local paper would run, I'm afraid,
                    but that's just as well). (*Say Goodnight* 50)

Perhaps to maximize contrast, Liu writes this rebellion in the classical "patriarchal" measure of blank verse. The one variation, two iambic trimeter lines at the midpoint and end of each of the poem's two twelve-line stanzas, contracts the meter for emphasis, almost the way George Herbert, the poet-Anglican priest, did in devotional poems.

The "Father dear" addressed in the poem's second line may refer not only to the speaker's father but to a Mormon priest, a representative of institutional prescriptions and proscriptions that Liu embraced to the point of getting interested in missionary work before he came to the realization that his homosexuality ruled out adherence to Mormon practice and doctrine. (See Liu and Tabios, pp. 70–74.) Even "God the Father" could be invoked. And one might also read the word "dear" as ambiguous if it represents the high cost of dealing with authority figures for the gay man as much as an archly uttered endearment.

The son's graphic reporting about his cavity being "invaded" and the assertion that it happens publicly seems intended to invade the father's consciousness. There are such aggressive words as "hooks" and "crack," the latter also suggesting a flaw or fragmentation. Assonance linking the final words in the first and fourth lines, to some extent, "elastic" in the third, and the existence of "ass" in "classified" helps Liu mock "polite society," exemplified by "our local paper," which would keep this information about "ass-eating" "classified" and not allow it to "sully" a "classified ad," much less the news section. Yet, in its categorization of the sexual act described in the imagery, a structural metaphor—the "no" before "classified/ ad" negating its appearance in the "paper" but not its existence as a trope—*does* advertise the event, as though the two men involved are "selling" it as something others should "buy."

The first of two twelve-line stanzas continues:

> We met in a bar that's gay one night a week —
> teenage boys in cages, men on the floor,
> but that's not what you want to hear, is it?
> How he noses into my cheeks on callused knees,
> lip-synching to the rage of techno-pop,
> that ecstasy of spit. (*Say Goodnight* 50)

The bar music's "rage" is not only about its current popularity but about fury against condemnation of the sexual practices detailed or homosexuality in general. A reader can sense this behind the previous pseudo-genteel tone ("I'm afraid"; "but that's just as well") and matter-of-fact presentation of imagery. Either "father" that I have mentioned may stand as a synecdoche for any homophobic reader and perhaps even assimilation-oriented gay men who criticize other gays for such activities as "ass-eating."

The poem was probably written around the time of the debate involving the "Don't Ask; Don't Tell" policy established in 1994 (and not repealed until 2011). This "official federal policy on military service by lesbian, gay and bisexual individuals" entailed "discrimination in its purest form and prevented service members from being openly queer without threat of being discharged," because the military leadership assumed "that the presence of LGBTQ individuals in any branch ... would undermine the ability of people to carry out their duties" ("Repeal of 'Don't Ask, Don't Tell'"). The policy resulted in "thousands" of discharges. The "prodigal son" in the poem takes aim at social imposition of gay invisibility by engaging in unabashed imagistic representation, seemingly transgression for the sake of empowerment that visibility may confer. The poem's second half complicates matters:

> He's after me to shit into his hands.
> What should I say? (I told him I'm afraid
> he'd only smear it across my wide-eyed face,
> hard as it is to tell you this.) How plans
> have gone awry is more than apparent here –
> this sty he calls a home

tender as a mattress filled with our breath,
our sex unsafe. *Oh stay with me*, he croons,
my eyes clenched shut, head trying not to flinch
as he makes the sign of the cross on my chest
with a stream of steaming piss, asking me
         if we were born for this. (50)

The speaker ironically makes the paternal addressee an active participant in the event by pretending to ask how to respond to the lover's masochistic desire. He confesses that the lover's masochistic reception could turn into a sadistic gesture. It may cross the threshold of injury ("our sex unsafe") and humiliation for him. Even if the question to the "father" in the second line is mockery, a fake call for advice, it is also serious—in the sense that it is addressed to the speaker himself and is answered right away.

Readers will differ about whether this passage marks a limit to and critique of transgression. If it is not merely viewed as an ironic pose or an easy pun on "hard," the phrase, "hard as it is to tell you this"—part of a parenthetical passage that is thematically *central*—might have the connotation of religious confession. If the revelation is really difficult, could it be that the speaker feels guilty about transgression, and that admission would legitimize drawing a bold line between acceptable and unacceptable conduct (or even proper behavior and sin) regarding consensual sex? Whether the speaker is saying that his own as well as the father's "plans" for him "have gone awry" is not clarified. The reader can construe that the son, while cherishing "tenderness," has not planned to make a "sty" his "home" or to risk exposing himself to the possibility of physical harm. The phrase, "our sex unsafe," seems to confess that the lovers are acting irresponsibly in foregoing protection against HIV infection and other maladies.

On the other hand, an interpreter who maintains that the poem validates transgression can argue that the speaker finds it difficult "to tell you this" because of the reasonable fear of rejection by the actual father, demonization by the clergy, and persecution by homophobic political forces influenced by religious institutions—rather than because of shame about a confessed "sin." For those who have read enough of Liu's overtly politicized poetry about gay experience to make connections between poems, "how plans have gone awry" could well register as deep anxiety and anger, about the impact of homophobia in US culture. To counterbalance this anxiety and anger, the narration of details is designed not only to defy but to vex the father, a synecdoche for all homophobes/heterosexists, and thus gain a form of revenge for oppression.

Students should be informed that the cross image near the end of the poem is most likely an allusion to Andres Serrano's "Immersion (Piss Christ)," a 1987 photograph of Jesus on a crucifix immersed in the artist's own urine. Serrano has always maintained that his intention was never anti-Christian. However, conservative members of the US Congress considered the work blasphemous and cited it, along with Robert Mapplethorpe's homoerotic photographs and several other artists' works that also won National Endowment for the Arts grants, as a reason to pass the "[Jesse] Helms Amendment" to slash NEA funding. (See Steven C. Dubin, *Arresting Images*, 175–180.) A reader could view the speaker's image of the lover's "sign of the cross" on [the former's] chest as a gesture of transgressive parody against homophobia in Christianity, or as a confession of shame that plays into the conservative Congressmen's charge of blasphemy, or as an implication of ambivalence.

Ironically, the speaker tells his "father," one half of the speaker's genetic origin, about the urinating lover's final question concerning origins—of his son's use of abjection in sexual behavior, or their gay identity. Paternity is no more of a qualification to answer the question (made ambiguous by the poem's final "this") than the lovers' possession of their own experience. The question of whether someone is born gay or becomes gay because of environmental factors can be seen as an attempt to push "confession," hence surveillance of gay identity to its (il)logical end-point. As Michel Foucault asserts about surveillance in general, a "total" explanatory framework, even if used to take the heat off gays, enables co-optation of transgression and an ability to regulate gays' experience and "help" them govern themselves according to that understanding. One can read the lover's final question as unwittingly reinforcing the poem's confessional element, or, instead, one could conclude that the speaker's saving this "big question" for last, where and when it cannot be answered, empties confession of force.

If "The Prodigal Son Writes Home" consisted of only the first stanza, I do not think that clashing overall interpretations would emerge, though advocates of gay "assimilation" and proponents of a "diversity" approach would put forth diverging *evaluations* of behaviors depicted. Whether one interprets the poem as the representation of the speaker's act of emancipatory transgression, of apologetic confession (of behavioral excess, if not homosexual practices in general), or of abiding ambivalence depends upon a reading of possible signs of anxiety and guilt in the second stanza. One could conclude that these signs halt the transgressive momentum of the first stanza and move the poem in the opposite direction, or that the drive for autonomy and liberation from heterosexist constraints outweighs and subdues the pull of guilt and self-doubt, or that the struggle between the two tendencies is unresolved.

Class discussion should concentrate on interpretation of the poem's language and thematic development before turning to evaluation of perceived ideological perspective, since the latter could divert readers from the specificity of the former. (Regarding potential homophobic responses to the poem, I put ground rules for discussion in my syllabi that set general standards of tolerance and prohibition of hate speech, and I devise ways of short-circuiting violations of those rules to avoid conflagrations.) Though it should be saved for last in both class discussion and a paper, students' focus on the intersection between their views on the assimilation/diversity conflict and their sense of Liu's presumed conscious or unconscious final intention should make for an engaging, strong conclusion to an essay on the poem.

The final example in this chapter is Sheila E. Murphy's "Now That" (2020). This short poem reflects enough "narrative incoherence" (discussed in my first chapter on difficulty, with Tabios's prose-poem "Come Knocking" as the example) to throw off readers who expect a seamless transition from one phrase, clause, or sentence to the next.

Disjunctive elements and complex troping are the main features that give rise to divergent readings of Murphy's poem. "Now That" consists of seven free-verse couplets with a gradual expansion of line length. The first two lines each have three or so accented syllables, whereas the last two have seven and six accented syllables respectively. Sentences beginning at the end of the third and fourth couplets are completed in the following ones. Despite the simplicity of diction, establishing a connection between the first two sentences, which are the first two couplets, is not simple:

> Now that I have something
> I have something to protect.
>
> This unwoven world may own
> moments in common or may not. (48)

The only obvious linkage between the two sentences are the verbs "have" and "own," which are attributed to the "I" (which, for now, I presume is the poem's speaker) and "this … world," respectively. "Have" can signify either possession of an object or being in contact with "something"/someone. Because of several words and phrases in later couplets, the "easiest" reading to pursue involves placing the opening "I" and "something" in the context of a love relationship. Like a sonnet, a form that has frequently featured the theme of love, this poem has fourteen lines, but it lacks rhyme and iambic pentameter and has a seven-stanza division.

"This unwoven world," the environment that actually serves as a space for the couple's positive experience of "common" interest, signified by the common metonymy "moments," is said to control that experience. The adjective "unwoven," an ontological metaphor for a fundamental attribute of the space, suggests a disunity of elements within it that makes the chance for "moments in common" uncertain. In attributing power to the space, the personification "own" implies that environmental factors could either facilitate or disrupt the speaker's efforts to work to achieve common ground with the other and thus to safeguard the relationship. "Now That" continues:

How do we connect when we do not
resemble? How might we derive a lesson

from a lesson not yet learned?
The earning of a heart refashions

something of a brain, an engine particled
into invisible détente allowed in keeping. (48)

The fact that the speaker uses the verb "resemble" without the expected "each other" can be explained as poetic shorthand, and "resemble" can signify aspects of physical appearance, character traits, or both. The enjambment that separates "not" and "resemble" and therefore emphasizes both words evokes a potential for alienation. The speaker hopes to discover whether (and if so, how) it is possible, despite differences, to turn the initial hint or manifestation of connection that allowed her to "have something" with the other person into a sustained connection. The second question implies that the awareness necessary to realize her objective must come from an as yet unlearned "lesson"—ostensibly about the causes of obstacles that have cropped up in the relationship and how to surmount them.

Perhaps responding somewhat obliquely in the next sentence to the questions, the speaker suggests with the noun "earning" that she had to labor to acquire the "something" ("heart") that she has, and then that this work itself alters "something" (the poem's third use of the word) about her cognitive processes. Given its association with clothing, the verb "refashions" seems less serious and more vulnerable to further transformation than "reconstructs" would be. The ontological metaphor "engine" emphasizes the labor and mobility of thinking, and "particled" indicates the division of the mind's operations, one of which makes the necessary adjustments of thinking, communication, and other actions to "allow" and then achieve "invisible détente" with the beloved in order to "keep" the relationship. This achievement is "invisible" if the other person does not know about the work that the speaker has done. However, the modifier "particled," along with the limiting term "something," indicates that other parts of the brain may be immune to "refashioning" and that cognitive dissonance could undermine efforts to "keep" what the speaker has "earned." The three anxious questions in the last two couplets evince doubt about whether "refashioning" can prevail over other (perhaps problematic) "particles" of thinking:

> As the moment freshens to another moment,
> how will we remember what we thought?
>
> And will it matter anymore? Will this point of thinking
> translate to another place from which to start? (48)

Harking back to the uncertainty about desired "moments in common" in the second couplet, the speaker marks the transition from one moment to the next as a potential danger zone, despite the positive connotation of the verb "freshens." A "refashioned" thought of connection can be "unwoven," displaced, and potentially rendered irretrievable by a thought that damages the couple's intimacy and makes it not "matter anymore." The noun "point" in the penultimate line can house several meanings: juncture in time and space, concept, dangerously sharp end of an object, such as a needle or corkscrew. In Murphy's concise personification, the point itself does the translating, but this represents the thinking that the two principals do from moment to moment. A "translation" may successfully match the original idea and emotional content or, instead, not correspond to the intention and thus bring about a change (depicted by the metonym "place") that marks an end and a beginning, whether positive or negative, from each of their perspectives. In the reading I've been entertaining, the poem concludes with the troubling uncertainty of unanswered questions about the speaker's ability to "protect" the "something" of the relationship she has "earned."

An alternative interpretation of "Now That" follows Roland Barthes's invitation to dispose of concern about authorial intention. For example, the reader should not presume that the "voice" speaking of possession and protection in the first couplet is the same as the one referring to "this unwoven world" as a possible possessor of "moments" in the second. Multiple voices might be questioning and responding to each other. To re-cite Barthes, examination of this text can attempt to "reach that point" that traces "where only language acts, 'performs,' and not ['Murphy']" (143).

In this reading, the "problem" that the object possessed in the opening couplet is not specified and is not resolved later in the poem; this lack of specification precludes (re)construction of a particular dramatic situation or a story with characters, though fragmentary narrative elements without firm contexts arise. "This ... world" registers as a generalized physical or conceptual space that lacks overall coherence ("weaving"). And one can read its personified "ownership" or inability to own the metonymic "moments [events] in common [of commonality]" as passive containment of causes and effects produced during the interaction of the elements and inhabitants of that "world." "Moments in common" could signify the similarity of discrete natural events, distinct from human beings taking action, as much as it could the sharing of common experiences by people.

The introduction of the pronoun "we" in the third couplet indicates a focus on human interaction in general and not on a limited number of people. The first question considers whether the narcissistic reassurance of resemblance is necessary for communicative connection, and the second wonders how a general "pedagogy" founded on experience can break through current failures to learn. "The earning of a heart" is ambiguous: though it can refer to gaining erotic love, it can also signify meriting the affection found in friendship *and* achieving the ability—through "refashioning" the "brain"—to feel and exhibit empathy for others *in general*. Similarly, one can construe "détente" as being between people, but also between warring thoughts, perhaps about connection with others versus autonomy, in a single mind. Although the strained syntax of the second clause in the fifth couplet (not acknowledged in the prior reading) poses a challenge to full comprehension, one can surmise, in the latter détente scenario, that a mental operation divides ("particles") a cluster of concepts ("something of a brain") into many parts to analyze their relations and then calms down consciousness either by achieving a reconciliation of differences or pragmatically directing one aspect to function in one context and others in other contexts.

Shifting from an account of the advantages of cognitive "refashioning," the final three questions of "Now That" are concerned with destabilization of thought and its impact. The questioner wants the movement of thought processes to have a positive cumulative effect—to enable a thinker to continue to profit from "a lesson" "derived" and maintain a useful "détente" between antagonistic forces. However, the insufficient capacity of memory (for someone who cannot go "backwards" as easily as a reader of a poem on a page can) to manage the flow of time might thwart this goal. Also, the "freshness" of new thinking can make a previous thought seem "stale." And continual displacement ("translate to another place") of "thinking" from "point" to point would constitute a ceaseless series of beginnings ("another place from which to start") which would make the thinker lose the benefits of continuity, such as the ability to "have" and "protect" "something," to create connection as opposed to disjunction, and to enjoy harmony, as effected by "détente." The implication of progress in the title "Now That" is ironically deflated by the end of the poem: "Now that I have something," I cannot necessarily build on my gain or continue to have it in the same way or, possibly, even continue to have it—if and when a new "now" comes along.

Both interpretations of "Now That" situate the text as a poetic distillation of thinking about relations among possession, protection (of equilibrium), connection, time, thinking, and discontinuity. Theoretical assumptions about intention and reading in general play a part in their differences, but so do readers' specific associations attributed to certain words and phrases, along with different impressions about "how ... we connect" sentences "when [they] do not [quite] resemble" each other or how we assess their lack of connection. In the first interpretation of the poem, elucidation of the specific context of a love relationship increases the potential for emotional identification and empathic involvement and may decrease emphasis on the meditative component, whereas, in the second, the meditative aspect dominates and offers different satisfactions.

I have separated the discussion of each example of a poem that yields multiple interpretations from all the others. However, one form of classroom activity provides some confirmation for Derrida's generalization, "Each text is a machine with multiple reading heads for other texts" ("Living On," 107). When students note commonalities and contrasts between successively or concurrently studied poems on the syllabus, it sometimes brings out an unexpectedly cogent reading of one or both. Let's say that a class encounters Alvarez's "The Therapist" directly after Yeats's "A Prayer for My Daughter." Remembering that the daughter has no voice in Yeats's poem may prompt students to think more quickly and intensely about the implications of the therapist in Alvarez's being quoted very little and depicted sparingly. This can help students arrive at more than one perspective about how the two characters in Alvarez's poem negotiate issues of authority, un/happiness, in/security, and external control/individual autonomy—issues that have just been addressed in Yeats's poem.

In the case of Ramanujan's "Death and the Good Citizen," prior analysis of one or two Early Modern poems can pave the way for a successful treatment of the complex workings of metonymy, which figure the "recycling" of body parts as a displacement of human identity that "enables" its "survival." Relying on synecdoche and metonymy, the speaker in John Donne's "The Flea" (in)famously confects a pseudo-logical argument designed to trick a woman into premarital sex. He insists that the blood-sucking flea that had latched onto both of them has incorporated each of their identities and united them, as matrimony and sexual union do:

Mark but this flea, and mark in this,
How little that which thou deniest me is;
It sucked me first, and now sucks thee,
And in this flea our two bloods mingled be;
Thout know'st that this cannot be said
A sin, nor shame, nor loss of maidenhead,
Yet this enjoys before it woo,
And pampered swells with one blood made of two,
And this, alas, is more than we would do. (59)

Many readers have glossed the third and fourth lines as a manipulative allusion to the Christian symbolism of legally sanctioned marital intercourse. The speaker capitalizes on the fact that the "bloods" of such a couple are "mingled" in the child that their act produces. The verb "swells" in the penultimate line suggests that the flea is "pregnant" with the essence of the human couple. The speaker uses tropes in an even more outrageous way in the second stanza, in which he pretends to plead with the woman not to kill the flea. This sophist first declares that he and she are "almost, nay more than married" within the flea, and then, that the insect *is* their identity: "This flea is you and I, and this/ Our marriage bed, and marriage temple is ..." (59). He concludes the stanza with the wonderfully ridiculous image of the two of them "cloistered in these living walls of jet."

Ramanujan's speaker is addressing a situation in which the human beings "subjected" to displacement are dead, whereas Donne's man and woman are alive after the insect has allegedly "captured" their shared identity. So the "logic" implied by Donne's Lothario is that their identity exists, magically, both within themselves and in the flea. Despite differences between the rhetoric of the two poems, attention to the convoluted rhetorical gestures in Donne's poem can prepare students to understand its structural similarities with irrational components of how metonymy and synecdoche work in "Death and the Good Citizen."

Well-known ideas about human identity surviving physical death through metonymic displacement can be found in Shakespeare's "Procreation Sonnets." In Sonnet 6, the speaker advises the young man "to breed another thee," or even ten children:

> Then what could death do, if thou shouldst depart,
> Leaving thee living in posterity?
> Be not self-will'd, for thou art much too fair
> To be death's conquest and make worms thine heir. (1731)

As Emily E. Stockard puts it, this "procreative argument makes its last appearance in sonnets 15-17, a triad which introduces instead the poet's power to immortalize the young man whom he has come to love" by setting "two conventional methods for defeating mutability, procreation and poetry, in competition …" (470). She states that "Sonnet 18 shifts the terms of the problem of mutability so that poetry alone can provide the solution," since the poet sees "mutability as an inherent imperfection in nature," while poetry has a "superior ability to render the youth's beauty eternal" (471). After lamenting that "summer's lease hath all too short a date," Sonnet 18's speaker insists that the addressee's "eternal summer shall not fade/ … Nor shall death brag thou wander'st in his shade," because the "lines" of "this" poem confer immortality on the young man: "When in eternal lines to time thou grow'st:/ So long as men can breathe or eyes can see,/ So long lives this, and this gives life to thee" (1733). The consolation of posthumous fame, either in descendants' memory and worldly existence or in a work of art's representation of one's transient life, depends on the consoled person's belief in the transformation of his/her physical absence into a meaningful presence: a future "life" of which s/he can be proud while literally alive. Pride in this extension of existence—rather than satisfaction in how the continuation of a family line gives the benefit of life to others or how others can gain pleasure or edification from the art work—is the attitude that various "Procreation Sonnets" present as useful for the young man. A reader can contrast this perspective with that ascribed to Ramanujan's "good citizen," if s/he believes that the citizen's decision to let her/his body be "recycled" is a sign of the desire to be useful after death more than to "survive" death. In both cases, one must account for metonymy as the poetic device utilized to convey important aspects of meditation about death and its aftermath.

This kind of comparison and contrast is not only useful in group work and class discussion, but, if the structure of the course permits, an essay. I've found repeatedly in teaching an Introduction to Poetry course over the years that when I make sure to craft the prompt and/or lead the discussion of the prompt with a few somewhat specific hints about areas for comparison without foreclosing other possibilities, students will often come upon further insights about connections and divergences between poems as they work on their essays.

Conclusion

In a 1991 book chapter, Jeanne Fahnestock and Marie Secor identify several widely used "special topoi" of literary critical rhetoric, and they assert that all of them underscore an "assumption about the complexity of literature, as well as the origin of that complexity" (91). Their conclusions are based on a survey of critical articles published roughly a decade earlier. A brief examination of how these and a fewer other topoi function and how they might be modified or work alternatively will help me emphasize some of my main points in the preceding chapters.

Fahnestock and Secor's first topos, "appearance/reality," involves the distinction between what is "obvious" and what needs to be discovered and is often represented by the orientational metaphorical pair of surface/depth (84–85). This will not surprise anyone. Since there is no more consensus on what constitutes "reality" than there is regarding "truth," the topos should be designated as appearance/"reality" (indicating *perception* of what is real) or as literal/figurative.

As suggested in my brief discussion of Stephen Best and Sharon Marcus's notion of "surface reading," an interpreter may find that some "surfaces" in a text do *not* warrant the probing of a hidden "depth," while many others do. Sometimes, an entire poem seems to posit appearance *as* the entire "reality." Many critics have used external evidence from William Carlos Williams's prose statements, which themselves require significant unpacking, and his affiliations with the Imagist and Objectivist movements to argue that many of his poems reflect an effort to render phenomenological perception in language. Analyzing the surface of William Carlos Williams's unpunctuated, single-fragment "Poem" (70), in which a simple narrative describes the movement of a cat, Peter Schmidt proves that, as central as the appearance/"reality" topos usually is to the reading of literary texts, one can occasionally interpret cogently without it. Not only does Schmidt substantiate how "with scientific accuracy Williams records one way cats have of walking" and how "the graceful economy of [the poem's] word-prints models a cat's gait," but he details how "syntax and line-breaks function as the equivalent of slow motion, and/or looking at film stills individually." Thus, Williams is providing two salient potential experiences for readers that "can't [be] perform[ed] simultaneously, only separately" (154). Further, he observes how the isolation of "sound patterns" create "intensely aural" as well as "visual" effects and how enjambments emphasizing prepositions "mark continuous motion across borders or barriers," just as the image-filled narrative does.

"Ubiquity," another topos discussed by Fahnestock and Secor, entails critics' tendency to spotlight some element, such as "a device, an image, a linguistic feature, a pattern" which has not previously been mentioned "and to find it everywhere"; "either the critic finds many examples of the same thing, or ... finds one thing in many forms, up and down a scale of grandeur and abstraction" (87). Jahan Ramazani's analysis of regularities in A.K. Ramanujan's tropes to support his postcolonial reading of "Death and the Good Citizen" is a strong example of the second form of ubiquity. But aren't the words "ubiquity" and "everywhere" hyperbolic? It would be more accurate to call this topos repetition or motif. Also, even if someone is the first to see a pattern, another reader may attach a different and equally compelling significance to it. Such disagreement will often stem from differing overall views about "reality" "behind" the poetic pattern's appearance. While enjoying aesthetic pleasure derived from repetition, members of a literature class can ponder the relative persuasiveness of divergent accounts of its thematic significance.

Fahnestock and Secor define "paradigm" as a "template fitted over the details of a literary text to endow them with order." They identify "a microparadigm" as "a small structural unit ..., which becomes the center of ever-larger concentric applications," and "a macroparadigm," which features the argument that "a recognizable set of relationships" (89) external to the text demonstrates a coherence to be found in the work. For example, Louis L. Martz's contention in *The Poetry of Meditation* (1954) that the structure of the spiritual exercises of St. Ignatius of Loyola and later Jesuits provides the structure for much seventeenth-century British devotional verse has had an enduring impact on how this poetry has been read.

Application of a critical theory's structure of inquiry to a poem is a major example of the use of a macroparadigm. When my classes entertain clashing interpretations of poems based on differing theories, I try to encourage openness to the explanatory power of macroparadigms and attention to what salient interpretive possibilities any of them leave out. But there is also the chance that two readers who utilize roughly the same macroparadigm will not come up with similar findings. For example, a feminist critic of Yeats's "A Prayer for My Daughter" like Joyce Carol Oates looks for possible signs of patriarchal ideology and finds only such signs, whereas another feminist like Elizabeth Cullingford might detect the same masculinist rhetoric but alongside egalitarian rhetoric. And my treatment of Timothy Liu's "The Prodigal Son Writes Home" suggests that two queer theorists have very different evaluations of the speaker's discourse based on differing strategies for strengthening queer visibility and empowerment.

Fahnestock and Secor's fourth topos is paradox, "unification of apparently irreconcilable opposites in a single startling dualism" (87). Their choice of term does not indicate an acknowledgment of how poststructuralist thought was already becoming influential in the late seventies in US literary academic culture and has challenged the New Critical *paradigm* of paradoxical unity. Unfortunately, "binary opposition" is a clunkier term, yet, since it is more apt and inclusive, I sometimes use it in a class. As my discussion of Alvarez's "The Therapist" indicates, I find it worthwhile to help students become alert to areas where hierarchical binary opposition, deconstruction of such oppositions, paradox, and demystification of paradox are prominent. (At times, ternary oppositions, such as Freud's id/ego/superego, are relevant.)

In transgender poetry, presumptions about paradox are stringently tested. In a poetics statement for the 2013 *Troubling the Line: Trans & Genderqueer Poetry & Poetics*, the first such anthology (which she co-edited), Trace Peterson suggests that the contemplation of the conventional gender binary should not be reduced to a neat paradox, just as individual identity cannot be isolated from contexts that impinge on a trans individual's existence in the world:

> Identity is in play in my work as one of a number of subjects, part of a number of discourses present ... .[It] is part of the world from which the poem arose, and the world that the poem creates. It is not banned, all the violence of it is present, but as a writing subject, I am different from moment to moment, not trapped by it. (475)

In the long poem "Trans Figures" (2007), Peterson describes transgender people's need to develop strategies to respond to cis-gender incomprehension and marginalization. This implies how unlikely it is that the allegedly reassuring reconciliation of paradox could be achieved. Note the unsettling use of synecdoche and the wordplay of "trial" and "tries":

> The voice
> is not built like other bodies that do this,
> driving around at night ... .
>   Sometimes the car in the next lane
> slows down, because it saw something unusual.
> The voice is very conscious of efforts to pass
> this trial, tries on gestures that will get it
> overlooked, a gentle throwing back of the hair
> it saw someone do who was a real body, a bending
> forward in the seat so it will seem
> for an instant, like that someone is living in its skin. (*Since I Moved In*, 15)

These lines respond cogently to Judith Butler's question, "Does being female constitute a 'natural fact' or a cultural performance, or is 'naturalness' constituted through discursively constrained performative acts that produce the body through and within the categories of sex?" (x). Peterson foregrounds both the performative aspects of gender construction and *reconstruction and*, implicitly, the disjunction between "a real body" and a person's emotions and cognitions pertaining to self-identification. Binary opposition is a structure that can help a reader begin to address this complex subject matter, but the opposition's stability will not remain intact by the end of the analysis.

In a 2009 article that surveys literary interpretations published near the turn of the millennium, Laura Wilder and Joanna Wolfe report that the four topoi that I have discussed above "continue to be invoked" (175). They add, however, that Wilder (in a 2005 essay) concludes that one more cited by Fahnestock and Secor, "*contemptus mundi*, in which the critic assumes despair over the condition of society," is less evident and has been "replaced by a topos that redirects despair into hope for social justice." The critic assumes a "connection between literature and our present condition" and "seeks avenues toward social change" (175). As my readers know, long before this mainstream "replacement," politically emancipatory endeavors have been the main impetus for African-American literature and criticism. The Black Arts movement of the 1960s particularly exemplifies the priority given to this topos. The same can be said for the Feminist criticism of the time, as well as Marxist analysis, commentary on the literature of Native Americans, Chicanos, Asian Americans, and texts about gay and lesbian literature. In examining a poem's representation of power relations and various attitudes toward social conditions ascribed to authorial intention or otherwise located in the text, critics deploying the "social justice" topos do not always "redirect despair into hope" but engage in critique. This gesture has the potential to move an audience to pursue further resistance to oppression that in turn could serve as a basis for hope.

One question is how reparation, discussed earlier in connection with Eve Kosofsky Sedgwick's essay, fits or doesn't fit the "social justice" topos. Sometimes critique and reparation flow together in the same poem. For example, in Gwendolyn Brooks's "Langston Hughes," it is hard to separate celebration of the senior poet as an inspiriting role model from tropes that allude to the oppression against which Hughes battled. Given that those who struggle against injustice frequently take a long time to achieve their aims, as seen in the treatment of Frederick Douglass and Barack Obama in Shockley's "(mis)takes one to know one," I would suggest that many reparative gestures in poetry do not *primarily* function as part of the effort to overcome oppression (e.g., through critique). Instead, they cultivate positive affect that promotes and sustains individual and collective psychological well-being (and, as Sedgwick points out, hope) despite harsh social conditions. It is a moot point whether reparation should be classified as a separate topos from "social justice"; in any case, it deserves attention whenever it surfaces in poetry. As I suggested earlier in reference to Liu and Yeats's poems, thinking about how the positive and problematic aspects of reparation for people's psychological and political health are disclosed in poems is a valuable activity.

On the basis of Wilder's 2005 findings, Wilder and Wolfe add "two new topoi … which reflect the attention recent criticism pays to the social and historical contexts" (175) of literature and scholarship on it. One of these, which is intimately connected with allusion, is "context" as "a variant of the paradigm topos" in which "the critic" brings "historical and contextual detail … to bear on textual interpretation." Critics writing during the first two-thirds of the twentieth century were obligated to apply historical context to the study of literary works that alluded directly to sociopolitical events and trends. The difference that Wilder and Wolfe find is that, since the advent of the New Historicism, Postcolonialism, and Cultural Studies, elucidation of context is widely considered crucial for *any* text. Without particulars of historical context, those for whom the "social justice" topos is central would probably have to fall back on inadequate, relatively vague generalizations drawn from political philosophy or common parlance, and their observations of "depth" beneath a poem's "surface" might seem arbitrary.

Differences among readings sometimes pivot on contrasts in the assignment of historical contexts, including aesthetic ones, as relevant or irrelevant to particular poems. (Recall, for instance, Vanita and Cullingford's extremely different assessments of context in "A Prayer for My Daughter.") Referring to the recent trend of global modernist studies, Christopher Bush notes that "the very idea of the global implies new conceptions of history so unimaginably vast and complex that" they are not reliable in "perform[ing] their traditional function of explanatory, clarifying context," so "'context' … comes to function … as the inadequately singular name of an ever-receding horizon, a problem rather than a solution" (76). Bush does not see "interpretation" as "a question of reducing" a text to context "or restoring" context to the text "but of what is brought to bear and what is not: a composite of inclusions and exclusions, so no hermeneutic or ethical preference can be given a priori to either" (86). There is no "knowable original, naturalized textual condition" (88) to serve as a compass.

The history of scholarship on Emily Dickinson's poetry has confronted the *literal* absence of certainty about an original, authoritative textual state, given the existence of different versions, "letter-poems," and fragments. Dickinson scholarship has advanced by overcoming the suppression of particular contexts, such as the extremely close relationship between the poet and her sister-in-law, Susan Gilbert Dickinson—interpreted from the former's letters and their contemporaries' recollections. Dominique Zino traces "how our encounters with Dickinson's work, from the 1890s to the present moment, have been guided by our insatiable desire for immediacy" yet "by critical applications of strategies of hypermediacy and remediation" (33). According to Zino, whether a critic is "describing a poem in relation to emblem books or facsimiles in relation to encoded text, there are no pure raw materials that, in themselves, are foundational to interpreting texts—only emergent materialities." Faculty can send students to the Emily Dickinson Archive (edickinson.org) to speculate on whether the printed version that they have been given adequately represents what they discern in the reproduction of the poet's handwritten texts. They may discover that a poem that conformed to the quatrains in alternating tetrameter and trimeter that Dickinson learned from Calvinist hymns in one version actually reveals a different pattern of the poet's own making in another.

Differing views of context sometimes exert power beyond the academy. This happened when the Anti-Defamation League led a public outcry against Amiri Baraka's "Somebody Blew Up America," written a month after the September 11 attacks, and demanded that he be stripped of his position as New Jersey Poet Laureate. (The position was subsequently eliminated.) As Piotr Gwiazda notes, during this controversy, prominent European-American poets tended to support Baraka's First Amendment rights but did not counter and sometimes even reinforced the negative interpretation (480–483). The part of Baraka's long, anaphoric catalogue poem that the protesters focused on were lines criticizing the state of Israel. They placed the entire poem in the context of virulent anti-Semitism. Baraka asks: "Who know why Five Israelis was filming the explosion/ And cracking they sides at the notion/ … Who knew the World Trade Center was gonna get bombed/ Who told 4000 Israeli workers at the Twin Towers/ To stay home that day/ Why did Sharon stay away?"

In his response, "The ADL Smear Campaign against Me," Baraka argues that his foes' accusation of anti-Semitism is based on unfairly equating criticism of Israel with prejudice against Jews in general and on excluding deliberation about the poem's most significant context. The catalogue of "Somebody Blew Up America" names "various forces of terror Afro Americans and other oppressed people of the world have suffered, slavery colonialism, Imperialism, Neo neo-colonialism, National Oppression." And Baraka's critics ignore his allusions to "the creators of the holocaust, e.g. 'who put the Jews in ovens,/ and who helped them do it,/ Who said "America First"/ and Ok'd the yellow stars,' which … is a reference to America's domestic fascists just before World War II and the Nazi Holocaust." Baraka also cites "the poem's listing of some of the Jews across the world, oppressed, imprisoned, murdered by actual Anti-Semitic forces, open or disguised, such as Rosa Luxembourg, Liebneckt, and Julius and Ethel Rosenberg." In fact, the line, "Who killed the most Jews" comes directly after "Who killed the most niggers" and before "Who killed the most Italians." It is fair to say that the poem's detractors engage in contextual synecdoche: they act as though a relatively small part of the text is its essence, and this allows them to draw a frame around the entire text and ignore counterevidence.

Critics who follow Fredric Jameson's lead regard historicizing as an imperative of *all* literary interpretation that must dominate the process. But Christopher Bush wisely cautions that a contextual approach can "be wielded as a blunt instrument that effaces the specificity of any given text" (80). Imagine, for example, a reader insisting that Sheila Murphy's "Now That" reflects particular historical events or trends and losing the poem's repeated resistance to precise contextual framing. It is especially important, as Matthew Zapruder asserts, not to ignore how poetry affords "a space for the possibilities of language as material," allowing "language its inherent provisionality, uncertainty, and slippages" (12) and emphasizing "connections that are hidden when language is being used for another purpose" (13), such as a business transaction. When a poem exposes the "inherent limitation of the material of language—that words are imprecise in their relation to whatever" they refer to, this can emerge as "a place of communion" that imposition of a specific context could unfortunately disable.

Wilder and Wolfe's final topos "mistaken critic" (175)—an allusion to a text by Lucian of Somosata—is the same as Stanley Fish's point about the "remedial" function of every new reading that I cited at the beginning of my third chapter. Wilder and Wolfe especially align this "need of correction" of "previous critics" with the latter's inability to grasp the "reality" beyond the literary work's "appearance." There are good reasons to cringe at the adjective "mistaken" when applied to well-trained, erudite literary critics, but even some professionals are fallible enough to fall into what enough members of an interpretive community would regard as a self-contradictory, factually inaccurate, insufficiently specific, or arbitrarily partially focused reading. As for readers without substantial training in literary analysis, commentary on "Somebody Blew Up America" that relegates "the poem's larger preoccupation with how myths and lies influence historical events and determine human actions" (Gwiazda 469) to the periphery deserves to be called "mistaken criticism," primarily because the readers do not articulate how parts of the catalogue crucially relate to other parts (and, in fact, ignore those other parts) and they uncritically assume the validity of a metonymy linking Israel and all Jews.

Nevertheless, I would replace the term "mistaken critic" for Wilder and Wolfe's topos either with "alternative or mistaken reading" or just "alternative" (with the tacit possibility of "mistaken" included). After all, different critics can often achieve comparable levels of specificity, nuance, and coherence in supporting divergent claims about appearance/"reality," the significance of textual repetition, paradigm, deployment of binary oppositions, application of contexts, and social justice. Interpreters create plausible *conjectures*, partly because, as Bush suggests, context cannot be exhausted. After a thorough discussion of a text, various members of an intellectual community often will not reach consensus, yet an attitude of dialogic openness and a desire to enhance whatever understanding is possible is far preferable to the use of conversation to serve egotistical bids for dominance. When students address interpretive differences rooted in ideological disagreement, they can do so in an atmosphere devoid of ad hominem and ad feminam offensives.

The various topoi do not include a direct consideration of how a reader's emotional response intersects with literary interpretation. For example, Fahnestock and Secor speak of an "emphasis on high seriousness" and "didactic content" in criticism that does not "take any account of pleasure," one aspect of literature's emotional impact; in their examples, they did not find references to "the beauty or pleasing effects of the works under scrutiny" (94). They maintain, however, with apparent irony, that "the process of discovering paradigms, paradoxes, ubiquitous elements, complexities, realities behind appearance, and our disdain for this world must be in itself a pleasure" (95). In their article, which includes the results of the experiment they conducted to assess whether teaching the topoi in a Writing about Literature course is effective, Wilder and Wolfe only mention enjoyment (and not emotional response in general) as a variable they were testing for. They find "that instruction in disciplinary conventions does not interfere with students' abilities to enjoy literature in other, more personal ways" (190).

In treating the analysis of affect in readers of literature, Rita Felski frames it as a compensation for what is usually missing in academic interpretation. In a Writing about Literature or Introduction to Poetry course, focus on reparation in a poem as it connects with other topoi can ensure that the class is addressing emotional aspects of reading. A question for a low-stakes assignment about a poem can elicit causes and effects of students' identification, empathy, alienation, ambivalence, or apathy, and then the professor can paraphrase some responses to generate interest during an early phase of class discussion. Even during a late phase of discussion, the topic of affect can return either to prod or enhance analysis or to provide a useful counterpoint to a conversational trend heading toward bloodless dissection.

Throughout this book, I have implied that there are educational benefits of poetry interpretation for college students that go beyond an appreciation for literature and competence in this particular activity. In his aphoristic catalogue poem "The Truth in Pudding," Charles Bernstein declares the "the role of teaching poetry" "to sustain" rather than "override difficulty," because "resistance to easy assimilation might sustain our engagement with the poem and in the process provide aesthetic pleasure and intellectual challenge" (*Recalculating* 9). The pursuit of this kind of "intellectual challenge" might strengthen the ability to meet challenges in other disciplines and situations.

Through the tracking of allusions in poems, students can develop greater knowledge and fuller understanding of history and culture. Having grown up during the tragic involvement of the United States in the Vietnam War, I found it helpful for my students in the second decade of this century who didn't know much about it to read poems like Yusef Komunyakaa's "Hanoi Hannah" and gain some historical context from discussing the impact of allusions.

Enhanced vocabulary is another benefit of slogging through difficulty. Just about every semester, I have a few students who believe that the words at their disposal cannot adequately express the complexity of their thoughts. I can imagine (and perhaps should create!) a course in which poems with lucidly uncommon vocabulary by Emily Dickinson, Mei-mei Berssenbrugge, Mark Young, Fred Moten, Derek Walcott, and ecopoets Brenda Iijima and Ed Roberson appear on the syllabus. I imagine these dedicated students learning more than a few new words and gradually increasing confidence in expressing ideas on various subjects.

I believe that it is no small benefit when students grapple with ambiguity and semantic deviation and strive to spell out the logic of tropes, because these efforts can contribute to the enhancement of the linguistic imagination. Such imagination is not only valuable for those who want to become effective poets, novelists, or playwrights—or advertising copywriters, for that matter—but also anyone in a field where, in some circumstances, ordinary ways of saying things fail to do justice to the nuances of what they are supposed to represent or, worse, support the persistence of maladaptive communication patterns.

Tropes are often closely aligned with imagery, and an appreciation of images—including surreal ones—helps expand the *sensory* imagination. The strengthening of linguistic/sensory imagination can have a felicitous impact on students' creative *and* discursive writing, pursuit of the visual arts and architecture, and even scientific thought-experiments involving visualization.

When students learn to read syntactical deviations, such as those found in Paolo Javier's "Feeling Its Actual," as generative of alternative possibilities of signification rather than merely as "errors," the process can get them to think about syntactical and grammatical conventions that are violated and how they both enable and constrain forms of meaning. Thus, they don't have to be Linguistics majors to gain a greater appreciation for how language actually works rather than simply assuming that it is a "natural," "transparent" medium of communication.

Similarly, as the class confronts evidence of narrative incoherence in a poem, a professor can lead students to recognize conventional devices and structures (of coherent narration) that are absent from important parts of the text, as in Tabios's "Come Knocking" and Murphy's "Now That." These features are so common that most readers rarely notice them. Being aware of them and of the impact of their absence from a text can deepen understanding of how authors display intention and how they leave room for their audience to fill in gaps independently. This kind of metacognition also applies to situations where students initially have trouble recognizing a specific text as a poem and need to reflect on and consider modifying their presuppositions about poetry and other genres. By performing these kinds of metacognition, students gain experience that can probably prepare them for similar thought processes as they analyze discursive prose in political science, sociology, business, new media studies, philosophy, psychology, art history, and the history of science.

Thinking about multiple interpretations of a poem also encourages metacognition about context (including allusion/intertextuality), paradigm (including critical theory), and other special topoi that are not necessarily confined to literary study. This activity fosters, in fact, an overall engagement with "critical thinking," one of the prime general education goals of almost all colleges and universities. Critical thinking is frequently traced to John Dewey's notion of "reflective thinking," in which the identification "of a problem" is the starting point, followed by "the observation of conditions, the formation and rational elaboration of a suggested conclusion, and the active experimental testing" (177). In poetry interpretation, the "problem" is the fact that the text is not transparent "communication" and needs commentary. "The observation of conditions" involves scrutiny of the poem's "terrain," areas that are open to multiple perspectives; the "rational elaboration of [more than one] suggested" approach to reading and their "conclusion[s]" are subjected to "active experimental testing." Sometimes I lead the class through various sections of a poem while considering the different interpretations together at each stage; at other times, I have everyone move through one reading at a time before comparing and contrasting all of them. For longer poems, the first approach is probably more efficient, whereas for relatively short poems, the second is just as suitable.

Dewey calls for "an attitude of mind which actively welcomes suggestions and relevant information from all sides" (205), "an active disposition to welcome points of view hitherto alien; an active desire to entertain considerations which modify existing purposes" (206). With these points in mind, I don't try to prod each member of the class to arrive rapidly at a single reading of a poem on the basis of their tentative conjectures during the discussion. The analysis has no foregone conclusion, and summary at the end gives relatively equal weight to all alternatives so that students can arrive at their own views later—perhaps in an essay. Dewey emphasizes "willingness to let experiences accumulate and sink and ripen" and the ability to avoid rushing to "results" (207). To respect this process in teaching a Writing about Literature course, I don't attempt coverage of a great many poems in class. Instead, I facilitate the elaborate analysis of a relatively small, manageable number.

Through such a careful examination of various interpretive possibilities, students' essays are much more likely to feature a nuanced, complex thesis (or cluster of main points) than they would by conducting poetic analysis that sticks to one straight line of thesis-support throughout most of the process. Let's say, though, that when it's time to complete the essay, a student is torn between two readings that s/he finds equally persuasive *and* equally problematic. I'd maintain that, as long as the essay is highly specific about why no single reading deserves full approbation, a thesis that suspends judgment is much more honest than one resulting from a contrived or haphazard way of deciding. And regardless of what wraps up interpretation, or "finally" defers closure, or makes a tentative claim and then hints at new contexts for further inquiry, it is realistic and perhaps also anxiety-reducing for students and faculty to recognize the relative instability of all poetic interpretation. Why should we need to lament the inability of a reading to match the example of a mathematical proof? Is there really any danger in the 2020s that a reader would go to the opposite extreme and idealize some version of "sublime," vertiginous indeterminacy? Relatively open, patient interpretation can offer provisional, context-bound illuminations for an engaged community of readers and, potentially, those actively pursuing positive social transformation.

Acknowledgments

Copyright © 2004 by Julia Alvarez. From THE WOMAN I KEPT TO MYSELF, published by Algonquin Books of Chapel Hill. By permission of Susan Bergholz Literary Services, New York, and Lamy, NM. All rights reserved.

Excerpts from "This Poem" in *This Poem / What Speaks? / A Day* by Tom Beckett, copyright © 2008 by Tom Beckett. Reprinted by permission of Otoliths.

Excerpt from "Langston Hughes" by Gwendolyn Brooks. Reprinted by Consent of Brooks Permissions.

Grateful acknowledgment is made to Victoria Cox for her permission to quote from her translation of "Presence" by Rosario Castellanos in *The Ofi Press Magazine*, 2012.

"Egg Rolls" from *Two and Two* by Denise Duhamel, © 2005. Reprinted by permission of the University of Pittsburgh Press.

Grateful acknowledgment is made to Marsh Hawk Press for permission to quote from "Feeling Its Actual" from *The Feeling Is Actual*, copyright © 2011 by Paolo Javier.

"Hanoi Hannah" from *Pleasure Dome: New and Collected Poems* © 2001 by Yusef Komunyakaa. Published by Wesleyan University Press. Used by permission.

Timothy Liu, "The Prodigal Son Writes Home" from *Say Goodnight*. Copyright © 1998 by Timothy Liu. Reprinted with the permission of The Permissions Company, LLC on behalf of Copper Canyon Press, coppercanyonpress.org.

Grateful acknowledgment is made to Sheila E. Murphy and Luna Bisonte Prods for permission to quote from "Now That" from *Golden Milk* (Luna Bisonte Prods, 2020), copyright © 2020 by Sheila E. Murphy.

"Successive Deaths" from *Alphabet in the Park: Selected Poems* © 1990 by Adélia Prado, translated by Ellen Watson. Published by Wesleyan University. Used by permission.

Excerpts from "Death and the Good Citizen" from *The Collected Poems* by A.K. Ramanujan. Reproduced with permission of © Oxford University Press India 1995.

"my last modernist #4 (or, re-re-birth of a nation)" and "(mis)takes one to know one" from *the new black* © 2011 by Evie Shockley. Published by Wesleyan University. Used by permission.

Excerpt from "Museum" from POEMS NEW AND COLLECTED 1957–1997 by Wisława Szymborska, translated from the Polish by Stanislaw Baranczak and Clare Cavanaugh. English translation copyright © by HarperCollins Publishers LLC. Reprinted by permission of Mariner Books, an imprint of HarperCollins Publishers LLC. All rights reserved.

Grateful acknowledgment is made to Marsh Hawk Press for permission to quote from "Come Knocking" from *Reproductions of the Empty Flagpole,* copyright © 2002 by Eileen R. Tabios.

Grateful Acknowledgment is made to Calyx Press for permission to quote from "Crow Voices" from *Indian Singing in 20th Century America*, copyright © 1990 by Gail Tremblay.

Grateful acknowledgment is made to Geoffrey Young and Isolate Flecks for permission to quote Young's poem "The Way We Are" from *Click Here to Forget*.

My analysis of Tom Beckett's "This Poem" in the first chapter is a substantially revised version of a section of my essay "Problems of Context and the Will to Parsimony" in *Reading the Difficulties: Dialogues with Contemporary American Innovative Poetry*, which I edited with Judith Halden-Sullivan (University of Alabama Press, 2014). The treatment of Paolo Javier's "Feeling Its Actual" in that chapter is a revision of a portion of my essay "Cultural (Un)translatability: Gander, Javier, Miller" in *Talisman* 42, 2014. The analysis of Denise Duhamel's "Egg Rolls" in the second chapter is a revision of part of my essay "Reading Duhamel, Kocot, and Lease with Altieri's *The Particulars of Rapture*" in *Reconstruction: Studies in Contemporary Culture*, vol. 12, no. 4, 2013. In my third chapter, parts of the section on Evie Shockley's "(mis)takes to know one" reflect the discussion of that poem in "Questioning Modes of Renewal and Reconstruction," my review of Shockley's book *The New Black* in *Denver Quarterly*, vol. 46, no. 4, 2012, pp. 45–49.

I would like to express my gratitude to the administrators of LaGuardia Community College–City University of New York for a sabbatical fellowship leave for the 2020–2021 academic year that enabled me to write this book. I am also indebted to the guidance of Amy Martin, my editor at Bloomsbury, and other members of the staff. I also thank the four insightful readers whom Bloomsbury enlisted to evaluate my manuscript.

As a Princeton undergraduate, I benefited greatly from the teaching of A. Walton Litz, Richard Ludwig, Robert J. Wickenheiser, Jonathan Arac, Lawrence Danson, D.W. Robertson, Theodore Weiss, John Peck, Dannie Abse,

Richard Murphy, and Tim Scanlon. At Columbia University as an MA and PhD student, I was privileged to be taught by Paul A. Bové, George Stade, Michael Wood, David Shapiro, Edward W. Said, Carolyn Heilbrun, S.F. Johnson, and Edward W. Tayler, and to discuss poetry extensively with fellow graduate students John Chu, Siri Hustvedt, and Tenney Nathanson.

To many of my colleagues in the English Department at LaGuardia, I express my profound thanks for our lively discussions of pedagogy and literature. In terms of dialogues specifically about poetry, I am especially grateful to Allia Abdullah Matta, Olga Aksakalova, Tuzyline Jita Allan, Nancy Berke, Hayan Charara, Carrie Conners, Catherine Costa, J. Elizabeth Clark, Terry Cole, Tara Coleman, Kristen Gallagher, Carlos Hiraldo, Margaret Heath Johnson, Karlyn Koh, Jennifer Kwon Dobbs, Jack Lynch, Peter Nickowitz, Kimberly del Busto Ramirez, John Silva, Christopher Schmidt, Gordon Tapper, Eleanor Q. Tignor, Phyllis van Slyck, and Dominique Zino. I also want to thank my four superb Chairs, Daniel Lynch, Sandra Sellers Hanson, Gordon Tapper, and Linda Chandler. The critical insights of various students have also enriched my thinking about poetry over the last four decades.

Of course, to all my friends who are poets and/or critics and would require as many pages as my Works Cited to mention, please accept my deepest appreciation for your wonderful conversation and support over the years. I also want to express gratitude to Reverends Jisei Nagasaka, Daido Nakamoto, and Shinga Takikawa for being exemplary Nichiren Shoshu Buddhist teachers. And a profound thank you to Molly, Ari, and Maya.

Works Cited

Ackerman, Margaret B. "Why I Don't Teach Poetry." *The English Journal*, vol. 57, no. 7, 1968, pp. 999–1001.

Alleyne, Lauren K. "The Complexity of Being Human: An Interview with Yusef Komunyakaa." *The Fight and the Fiddle*, May 1, 2018.

Altieri, Charles. *The Particulars of Rapture: An Aesthetic of the Affects.* Cornell University Press, 2003.

Alvarez, Julia. *The Woman I Kept to Myself.* Algonquin, 2004.

Anzaldúa, Gloria E. *Borderlands/ La Frontera—The New Mestiza.* Aunt Lute, 1987.

Ashtor, Gila. "The Mis Diagnosis of Critique." *Criticism*, vol. 1, no. 2, Spring 2019, pp. 191–217.

Baer, William, "Still Negotiating with the Images: An Interview with Yusef Komunyakaa." *Kenyon Review*, vol. 20, no. ¾, Summer/Autumn 1998, pp. 5–20.

Baraka, Amiri. "The ADL Smear Campaign against Me." *CounterPunch*, October 7, 2002.

Baraka, Amiri. *Somebody Blew Up America.* Black Dot Press, 2001.

Barthes, Roland. *Image, Music, Text*, translated by Stephen Heath, Hill & Wang, 1977.

Beckett, Tom. *This Poem/ What Speaks?/ A Day.* Otoliths, 2008.

Bennett, Louise. *Selected Poems.* Sangster's Book Stores, 1983.

Bernstein, Charles. *Attack of the Difficult Poems.* University of Chicago Press, 2011.

Bernstein, Charles. *My Way: Speeches and Poems.* University of Chicago Press, 1999.

Bernstein, Charles. *Recalculating.* University of Chicago Press, 2013.

Best, Stephen and Sharon Marcus. "Surface Reading: An Introduction." *Representations*, vol. 108, no. 1, November 2009, pp. 1–21.

Bogel, Fredric V. *New Formalist Criticism: Theory and Practice.* Palgrave MacMillan, 2013.

Bredin, Hugh. "Metonymy." *Poetics Today*, vol. 5, no. 1, 1984, pp. 45–58.

Brooks, Gwendolyn. *Selected Poems.* Perennial, 1999.

Brooks, Gwendolyn, E. Ethelbert Miller, and Bourne St. Clair. "Gwendolyn Brooks on Langston Hughes." *The Langston Hughes Review*, vol. 15, no. 2, Winter 1997, pp. 92–109.

Brunton, James. "Whose (Meta)modernism?: Metamodernism, Race, and the Politics of Failure." *Journal of Modern Literature*, vol. 41, no. 3, Spring 2018, pp. 60–76.

Burt, Stephanie. *Don't Read Poetry*. Basic Books, 2019. December 21, 2017.

Bush, Christopher. "Context." *A New Vocabulary for Global Modernism*, edited by Eric Hayot and Rebecca Walkowitz, Columbia University Press, 2016, pp. 75–95.

Bushell, Sally. "Intention Revisited: Towards an Anglo-American 'Genetic Criticism.'" *Text*, vol. 17, 2005, pp. 55–91.

Butler, Judith. *Gender Trouble: Feminism and the Subversion of Identity*. Routledge, 1990.

Castellanos, Rosario. "Presence." translated by Victoria Cox, *The Ofi Press Magazine*, no. 49, 2012.

Castiglione, Davide. *Difficulty in Poetry: A Stylistic Model*. Palgrave Macmillan, 2019.

Creely, Edwin. "'Poetry Is Dying': Creating a (Re)new(ed) Pedagogical Vision for Teaching Poetry." *Australian Journal of Language and Literacy*, vol. 42, no. 2, 2019, pp. 116–27.

Cull, Ryan. "'Inexhaustible Splendor': Thylias Moss, Praise Poetry, and Racial Politics." *Melus*, vol. 41, no. 1, Spring 2016, pp. 125–47.

Cullingford, Elizabeth Butler. *Gender and History in Yeats's Love Poetry*. Cambridge University Press, 1993.

Darwish, Mahmoud. *Unfortunately, It Was Paradise: Selected Poems*, translated and edited by Munir Akash, Carolyn Forché, Siman Antoon, and Amira El-Zein, University of California Press, 2013, pp. 119–62.

Derrida, Jacques. *Of Grammatology*. 1967. Translated by Gayatri Chakravorty Spivak, Johns Hopkins University Press, 1976.

Derrida, Jacques. "Living On: Border Lines." translated by James Hulbert. *Deconstruction & Criticism*. Seabury, 1979, pp. 75–175.

Derrida, Jacques. *Margins of Philosophy*. 1972. Translated by Alan Bass, University of Chicago Press, 1982.

Derrida, Jacques. *Positions*, translated by Alan Bass, University of Chicago Press, 1981.

Dewey, John. *Democracy and Education: An Introduction to the Philosophy of Education*. Macmillan, 1916.

Dharwadker, Vinay. "Introduction." *Collected Poems* A.K. Ramanujan. Oxford University Press, 1995, pp. xvii–xxxviii.

Donne, John. *The Complete English Poems*, edited by A.J. Smith, Penguin, 1975.

Dubin, Stephen C. *Arresting Images: Impolitic Art and Uncivil Actions*, Routledge, 1992.

Duhamel, Denise. *Two and Two*. University of Pittsburgh Press, 2005.

Dyson, Michael Eric. "Michael Eric Dyson, Author, *The Black Presidency.*" *The Frontline Interviews*. PBS, January 17, 2017.

Empson, William. *Seven Types of Ambiguity*. Chatto & Windus, 1949.

Eschner, Kat. "How the 1970s Created Recycling as We Know It." *Smithsonian Magazine*, November 15, 2017.

Fahnestock, Jeanne and Marie Secor. "The Rhetoric of Literary Criticism." *Textual Dynamics of the Professions: Historical and Contemporary Studies of Writing in Professional Communities*, edited by Charles Bazerman and James Paradis, University of Wisconsin Press, 1991, pp. 76–96.

Felsenthal, Carol. "The Strange Tale of the First Woman to Run for President." *Politico Magazine*, April 9, 2015.

Felski, Rita. *Hooked: Art and Attachment*. University of Chicago Press, 2020.

Fergusson, Francis. "Introduction." *Aristotle's Poetics*, translated by S.H. Butcher, Hill and Wang, 1961, pp. 1–44.

Fetterly, Judith. *The Resisting Reader: A Feminist Approach to American Fiction*. Indiana University Press, 1978.

Fish, Stanley. *Is There a Text in This Class? The Authority of Interpretive Communities*. Harvard University Press, 1980.

Foucault, Michel. "What Is an Author?" translated by Josue V. Harrari. *The Foucault Reader*, edited by Paul Rabinow, Pantheon Books, 1984, pp. 101–20.

Gallop, Jane. "The Ethics of Reading: Close Encounters." *Journal of Curriculum Theorizing*, vol. 16, no. 3, Fall 2000, pp. 7–17.

Gallop, Jane. "The Historicization of Literary Studies and the Fate of Close Reading." *Profession*, 2007, pp. 181–6.

Ghaziani, Amin. "Post-Gay Collective Identity Construction." *Social Problems*, vol. 58, no. 1, February 2011, pp. 95–125.

Gioia, Dana. "Introduction." *The Best American Poetry 2018*, edited by Dana Gioia and David Lehman, Scribner, 2018, pp. xxiii–xxxii.

Golding, Alan. "Faking It New." *Modernism/modernity*, vol. 16, no. 3, September 2009, pp. 474–7.

Gordon, Noah Eli. *Inbox*. BlazeVox, 2006.

Gwiazda, Piotr. "The Aesthetics of Politics/ The Politics of Aesthetics: Amiri Baraka's Somebody Blew Up America." *Contemporary Literature*, vol. 45, no. 3, Fall 2004, pp. 460–85.

Hamamra, Bilal Twfiq and Sanaa Abusamra. "'What's in a Name?': The Aesthetics of Proper Name and Diasporic Identity in Mahmoud Darwish and Edward Said." *Interventions: International Journal of Postcolonial Studies*, vol. 22, no. 8, 2020, pp. 1065–78.

Hammer, Langdon. "Frank Bidart and the Tone of Contemporary Poetry." *Southwest Review*, vol. 87, no. 1, 2002, pp. 75–89.

Hancher, Michael. "Three Kinds of Intention." *MLN*, vol. 87, no. 7, December 1972, pp. 827–51.

Herbert, George. *Poems*. Knopf, 2004.

Jakobson, Roman. "The Metaphoric and Metonymic Poles." 1956. *The Norton Anthology of Theory and Criticism*, edited by Vincent B. Leitch, Norton, 2010, pp. 1152–6.

Javier, Paolo. *The Feeling Is Actual*. Marsh Hawk Press, 2011.

Jerng, Marc C. "Race in the Crucible of Literary Debate: A Response to Winfried Fluck." *American Literary History*, vol. 31, no. 2, Summer 2019, pp. 260–71.

Johnson, Barbara. *The Critical Difference: Essays in the Contemporary Rhetoric of Reading*. Johns Hopkins University Press, 1980.

Karr, Mary. "How to Read 'The Waste Land' So It Alters Your Soul." *The Chronicle of Higher Education*, vol. 47, no. 24, February 23, 2001.

Komunyakaa, Yusef. *Pleasure Dome: New and Collected Poems*. Wesleyan University Press, 2001.

Lacan, Jacques. *Écrits*. 1966. Translated by Bruce Fink, New York: Norton, 2006.

Lakoff, George and Mark Johnson. *Metaphors We Live By*. University of Chicago Press, 1980.

Langer, Emily. "Trinh Thi Ngo, North Vietnamese Propagandist Known as 'HanoiHannah' Dies." *Washington Post*, October 6, 2016.

Lazer, Hank. "Of Course Poetry Is Difficult/Poetry Is Not Difficult." *Reading the Difficulties: Dialogues with Contemporary American* Poetry, edited by Thomas Fink and Judith Halden-Sullivan, University of Alabama Press, 2014, pp. 28–40.

Lin, Tan. "Disco as Operating System, Part One." *Criticism*, vol. 50, no. 1, 2008, pp. 83–100.

Lin, Tan. "Plagiarism: A Response to Thomas Fink." *Otoliths*, vol.4, no. 3, August 2009.

Lin, Tan. *Plagiarism/Outsource*. Zasterle, 2008.

Liu, Timothy. *Say Goodnight*. Copper Canyon Press, 1998.

Liu, Timothy and Eileen Tabios. "Timothy Liu: Towards Redemption." *Black Lightning: Poetry-in-Progress*, Eileen Tabios, Asian American Writers Workshop,1998, pp. 69–107.

Lorde, Audre. *Collected Poems*. Norton, 1997.

Maddox, Brenda. *Yeats's Ghosts: The Secret Life of W.B. Yeats*. HarperCollins, 1999.

Martz, Louis L. *The Poetry of Meditation: A Study in English Religious Literature of the Seventeenth Century*. Yale University Press, 1954.

Morris, Daniel. *Not Born Digital: Poetics, Print Literacy, New Media*. Bloomsbury Academic, 2016.

Murphy, Sheila E. *Golden Milk*. Luna Bisonte Prods, 2020.

Nica, Marius. "Teaching Poetry to Undergraduate Students." *Procedia Social and Behavioral Sciences*, vol. 11, 2011, pp. 215–19.

Oates, Joyce Carol. "'At Least I Have Made a Woman out of Her': Images of Women in Twentieth-Century Literature." *The Georgia Review*, vol. 37, no. 1, Spring 1983, pp. 7–30.

Obama, Barack. *A Promised Land*. Crown, 2020.

Otter, Samuel. "An Aesthetics in All Things." *Representations*, vol. 104, no. 1, 2008, pp. 116–25.

Patterson, Annabel. "Intention." *Critical Terms for Literary Study*, edited by Frank Lentricchia and Thomas McLaughlin, University of Chicago Press, 1995, pp. 135–46.

Perloff, Marjorie. "Between Hatred and Desire: Sexuality and Subterfuge in 'A Prayer for My Daughter.'" *Yeats Annual*, vol. 7, no. 7, 1990, pp. 29–50.

Perloff, Marjorie. "Reconsidering Maud Gonne." *English Literature in Translation*, 1880-1920, vol. 61, no. 2, 2018, pp. 250–5.

Perloff, Marjorie. "'The Tradition of Myself': The Autobiographical Mode of Yeats."*Journal of Modern Literature*, vol. 4, no. 3, February 1975, pp. 529–73.

Peterson, Trace. "Channeling and [Im]possibility: A Poetics and Erotics." *Troubling the Line: Trans and Genderqueer Poetry and Poetics*, edited by T.C. Tolbert and Trace Peterson, Nightboat Books, 2013, pp. 475–7.

Peterson, Trace. *Since I Moved in*. Chax, 2007.

Prado, Adélia. *The Alphabet in the Park: Selected Poems*, translated by Ellen Watson, Wesleyan University Press, 1990.

Ramanujan, A.K. *Collected Poems*. Oxford University Press, 1995.

Ramazani, Jahan. *The Hybrid Muse: Postcolonial Poetry in English*. University of Chicago Press, 2001.

Regan, Stephen. "Yeats, Nationalism and Post-Colonial Theory." *Nordic Irish Studies*, vol. 5, 2006, pp. 87–99.

Reid, David. "Euro-Scepticism: Thoughts on Metonymy." *University of Toronto Quarterly*, vol. 73, no. 3, Summer 2004, pp. 916–33.

"Repeal of 'Don't Ask, Don't Tell.'" *Human Rights Campaign*, 2020.

Rich, Adrienne. *The Dream of a Common Language*. Norton, 1978.

Saddlemyer, Ann. "Anne Butler Yeats." *Dictionary of Irish Biography*. Royal Irish Academy, nd. dib.cambridge.org.

Saddlemyer, Ann. "Designing Ladies: Women Artists and the Early Abbey Stage." *Princeton University Library Chronicle*, vol. 68, Winter 2007, pp. 163–200.

Schmidt, Peter. "'Animal Spirits.'" *Williams Carlos Williams Review*, vol. 33, nos. 1–2, 2016, pp. 147–71.

Sedgwick, Eve Kosofsky. *Touching Feeling: Affective, Pedagogy, Performativity*, edited by Michele Barale, Jonathan Goldberg, and Michael Moon, Duke University Press, 2003.

Seidel, Frederick. "An Interview with Robert Lowell." 1961. *Robert Lowell: A Collection of Critical Essays*, edited by Thomas Parkinson, Prentice Hall, 1968, pp. 12–35.

Shakespeare, William. *The Complete Signet Classic Shakespeare*. Harcourt Brace Jovanovich, 1972.

Shepherd, Reginald. "On Difficulty in Poetry." *Association of Writers and Writing Programs* Magazine, May/Summer 2008.

Shockley, Evie. *The New Black*. Wesleyan University Press, 2011.

Silliman, Ron. *The New Sentence*. Roof Books, 1987.

Steiner, George. "On Difficulty." *The Journal of Aesthetics and Art Criticism*, vol. 36, no. 3, Spring 1978, pp. 263–76.

Stockard, Emily E. "Patterns of Consolation in Shakespeare's Sonnets 1–126." *Studies In Philology*, vol. 94, no. 4, Autumn, 1997, pp. 465–93.

Szymborska, Wisława. *Poems New and Collected 1957–1997*, translated by Stanisław Barańczak and Clare Cavanagh, Harcourt, 1998.

Tabios, Eileen R. *Reproductions of the Empty Flagpole*. Marsh Hawk Press, 2002.

Tabios, Eileen R. and John Bloomberg-Rissman. "John Bloomberg-Rissman Interviews Eileen R. Tabios." 2014. *Against Misathropy: A Life in Poetry (2015–1995)*. Eileen R. Tabios. BlazeVOX Books, 2015, pp. 19–38.

Tabios, Eileen R. and Purvi Shah. "Eileen Tabios Interview." 2000. *Against Misathropy: A Life in Poetry (2015–1995)*. Eileen R. Tabios. BlazeVOX Books, 2015, pp. 146–60.

Tabios, Eileen R. and Tom Beckett. "Eileen Tabios." 2005. *E-x-c-h-a-n-ge-v-a-l-u-e-s: The First XI Interviews*, edited by Tom Beckett. Otoliths, 2007, pp. 89–107.

Torrelas, Lusvic. "Teaching Poetry through the Application of the Strategies Which Respond to Statements Made in the Communicative, Natural, and Multiple Intelligences Approaches." *Leanguas Modernas*, vol. 46, Segundo Semestre, 2015, pp. 105–22.

Tremblay, Gail. *Indian Singing in 20th Century America*. Calyx Books, 1990.

Vanita, Ruth. "Self-Delighting Soul: A Reading of Yeats's 'A Prayer for My Daughter' in the Light of Indian Philosophy." *Connotations*, vol. 24, no. 2, 2014/2015, pp. 239–57.

Voigt, Ellen Bryant. *The Flexible Lyric*. University of Georgia Press, 1999.

Watson, Ellen. "Introduction." *The Alphabet in the Park: Selected Poems of Adelia Prado*, translated by Ellen Watson, Wesleyan University Press, 1990, pp. vii–xiv.

West, Cornel. "Pity the Sad Legacy of Barack Obama." *The Guardian*, January 9, 2017.

West, Cornel. "President Obama and the Crisis of Black America: Interview with Cornel West." *New Politics*, 2012.

Wilder, Laura and Joanna Wolfe. "Sharing the Tacit Rhetorical Knowledge of the Literary Scholars: The Effects of Making Disciplinary Conventions Explicit in Undergraduate Writing about Literature Courses." *Research in the Teaching of English*, vol. 44, no. 2, November 2009, pp. 170–209.

Wilkinson, Joshua Marie. "On Poetry and Accessibility." *Evening Will Come*, vol. 3, no.11, March 2013.

Williams, William Carlos. *Selected Poems*, edited by Charles Tomlinson, New Directions, 1985.

Wimsatt, William K. Jr. "Genesis: Fallacy Revisited." *The Disciplines of Criticism*, edited by Peter Demetz, Thomas Greene, and Lowery Nelson, Jr., Yale University Press, 1968, pp. 116–38.

Wimsatt, William K. Jr. and Monroe C. Beardsley. *The Verbal Icon: Studies in the Meaning of Poetry*. University of Kentucky Press, 1954.

Wolfson, Susan J. "What Good Is Formalist Criticism? Or; 'Forms' and 'Storms' and the Critical Register of Romantic Poetry." *Studies in Romanticism*, vol 37, no. 1, Spring 1998, pp. 77–94.

Yau, John. *The United States of Jasper Johns*. Zoland, 1996.

Yeats, William Butler. *Michael Robartes and the Dancer*. Cuala Press, 1921.

Young, Geoffrey. *Click Here to Forget*. Isolate Flecks, 2016.

Young, Mary Alice. "High School English Teachers' Experiences with Poetry Pedagogy." Doctoral Thesis, Northeastern University School of Professional Studies, March 2016.

Zapruder, Matthew. *Why Poetry*. Ecco, 2017.

Zino, Dominique. "'The Invisible Hand of the Lyric: Emily Dickinson's Hypermediated Manuscripts and the Debate over Genre." *Textual Cultures*, vol. 10, no. 1, Winter 2016, pp. 1–36.

Index